Little Dorrit's SHADOWS

BRIAN ROSENBERG

Little Dorrit's
SHADOWS

Character and Contradiction in Dickens

UNIVERSITY OF MISSOURI PRESS
COLUMBIA & LONDON

Copyright © 1996 by
The Curators of the University of Missouri
University of Missouri Press, Columbia, Missouri 65201
Printed and bound in the United States of America

5 4 3 2 1   00 99 98 97 96

Library of Congress Cataloging-in-Publication Data

Rosenberg, Brian, 1955–
    Little Dorrit's shadows : character and contradiction in Dickens /
Brian Rosenberg.
        p. cm.
    Includes bibliographical references and index.
    ISBN 0-8262-1058-9 (alk. paper)
    1. Dickens, Charles, 1812–1870—Characters. 2. Characters and
characteristics in literature. 3. Dickens, Charles, 1812–1870. Little
Dorrit. 4. Contradiction in literature. 5. Fiction—Technique. I. Title.
PR4589.R6 1996
823'.8—dc20   96-2317
                                                                CIP

∞This paper meets the requirements of the
American National Standard for Permanence of Paper
for Printed Library Materials, Z39.48, 1984.

Designer: Stacia Schaefer
Jacket Designer: Susan Ferber
Typesetter: BOOKCOMP
Printer and binder: Thomson-Shore, Inc.
Typefaces: Sabon, Cochin, Casablanca, Woodtype Ornaments

For Eugene and Dena Rosenberg,
with love

CONTENTS

ACKNOWLEDGMENTS

FOR A SHORT BOOK, this one has had a long history, and so I have accumulated during the period of its creation a good number of debts. At Cornell, my reading of and writing about novels were shaped beneficially by Tom Jeffers; at Columbia, Steven Marcus, John Rosenberg, and John Romano carefully guided my work on Dickens through both a master's essay and a dissertation; at Allegheny College, my colleagues, my students, and the administration have always been warmly supportive. I would like to thank in particular David Miller and Susan Slote, for reading all or part of this manuscript, and Diane Goodman, Lloyd Michaels, Laura Quinn, Ben Slote, and Jim Bulman, for providing more general emotional and psychological support. Portions of the book were written while on a sabbatical leave endorsed by the college's Faculty Development Committee. Everyone at the University of Missouri Press has been exceptionally helpful and efficient; special thanks are due to William Holtz, for providing the most generous reading imaginable. To Jim Kincaid, for his unflagging encouragement and unmerited praise, I owe more than I can hope to repay. He's been this book's guardian angel—I'm tempted to say its Little Mother, though he's too tall by half to play the part and doesn't naturally have the temperament for it.

As always, my deepest gratitude is owed to my family and especially to my wife Carol, who provides the most important support for all that I do. She's also provided my own two characters, Adam and Sam. I can't honestly say that their energetic presence has made the writing of this book any easier or faster—but oh, what larks!

Earlier versions of portions of this manuscript have previously appeared as "Character and Contradiction in Dickens" in *Nineteenth-Century Literature* 47 (1992): 145–63; as "Character and the Demands of Structure: The Example of Dickens" in *The CEA Critic* 51 (1989): 42–54; and as "Vision into Language: The Style of Dickens's Characterization" in *Dickens Quarterly* 2 (1985): 115–24. My thanks to all three publications for permission to use this material.

A Note on Texts and Abbreviations

All quotations from Dickens's novels, stories, and essays are drawn from the Oxford Illustrated edition of his works (London: Oxford University Press, 1948–1958). Since the more authoritative Clarendon editions are not yet available for all Dickens's novels, I have made this choice for the sake of consistency and ease of reference.

The following abbreviations are used to refer to particular texts.

BR	*Barnaby Rudge*
CB	*Christmas Books*
DC	*David Copperfield*
DS	*Dombey and Son*
ED	*The Mystery of Edwin Drood*
GE	*Great Expectations*
LD	*Little Dorrit*
MC	*Martin Chuzzlewit*
NN	*Nicholas Nickleby*
OCS	*The Old Curiosity Shop*
OMF	*Our Mutual Friend*
OT	*Oliver Twist*
PP	*Pickwick Papers*
SB	*Sketches by Boz*
TTC	*A Tale of Two Cities*
UC	*The Uncommercial Traveller and Reprinted Pieces*

Little Dorrit's SHADOWS

INTRODUCTION

C HARACTER IN CONTEMPORARY LITERARY THEORY has typically become "character," just as real has become "real" and meaning "meaning." The term is used because it has historical significance and because no other easily replaces it (how often can one say "group of predicates"?),[1] but it is used slyly, as if according to a tacit agreement between writer and reader that both know better than to believe that such a chimera actually exists. This presents a problem, obviously, to one setting out to consider the representation of character by Dickens or by any other author. Studies of plot or politics or historical context may enmesh one in debates about *what* those things are but not in debates about *if* they are. Those who write about character today are often seen, like Wordsworth's Pagan, as stubborn adherents to a "creed outworn," and have been genially likened by William Gass to writers "about God, his cohorts, and the fallen angels."[2] The basis of such activity is not reason, certainly not rigorous method, but quixotic if rather touching faith.

I may exaggerate here, but only slightly. The truth is that the most fundamental premise upon which studies of character are based—that character exists to be studied—is often greeted today with skepticism or even hostility, since it has become associated with certain "limited civil and ethical ideologies" that carry controversial political weight.[3] One seldom hears such traditional literary terms as "symbol" and "theme" called imprisoning, as Hélène Cixous and others have called character,[4] and not since cries of the "death of the author" has an aspect of literature so frequently been declared moribund. The trick for anyone trying to discuss characterization, therefore, is to strike a balance between ignoring challenges to the enterprise on the one hand

1. Jonathan Culler, *Structuralist Poetics: Structuralism, Linguistics, and the Study of Literature,* 235.
2. William Gass, *Fiction and the Figures of Life,* 39.
3. Warner Berthoff, " 'Our Means Will Make Us Means': Character as Virtue in *Hamlet* and *All's Well,*" 322.
4. See Hélène Cixous, "The Character of 'Character,' " 387.

and endlessly whining about them on the other. To ignore them is to open oneself to charges of naïveté—a damning accusation these days—and outdatedness; to respond endlessly is to appear to protest too much and to leave little room for actual discussions of character itself. Besides, one is unlikely to change anyone's mind about so fundamental a theoretical issue: those who do not believe character exists will probably not be convinced by a study of character that it does, any more than a Republican will be swayed by the rhetoric at a Democratic convention.

My main purpose in this book is to consider, through intensive reading of one novel and more selective reading of others, the way Dickens imagines character and the representation of character; to identify stylistic, structural, and imagistic habits that mark his characterization; and to describe the typical effects of that characterization on the reader. Despite all the work done on Dickens during the past century and a half, there seem to me several important aspects of his characterization that have received inadequate or misguided attention, for reasons having to do with Dickens's effective if misleading shaping of his own image and with critical approaches insufficiently attuned to his methods. This consideration of Dickens, however, must necessarily be accompanied by reflection on some larger questions related to character and representation. When I began to write about Dickens's characters as a student in the mid-1970s, the most influential study of character was still probably E. M. Forster's *Aspects of the Novel* (1927), and the most highly regarded recent study was W. J. Harvey's *Character and the Novel* (1965). While the challenges to character proposed by Tzvetan Todorov, Roland Barthes, Cixous, and others were available and beginning to be considered, the most widely cited attacks on character remained those launched by the New Critics, F. R. Leavis, and José Ortega y Gasset. Such attacks appear, by present standards, mere skirmishes, and allowed most critics in 1975 to use such terms as "believable" and "rounded" with only slightly more self-consciousness than critics in 1950. Discussions of the characters of individual authors (if not of characterization generally) were frequent and not typically defensive.

That this has changed needs no demonstration, and why it has changed is obvious to anyone even passingly familiar with the recent evolutions in literary theory. The full effects and benefits of this change are open to some discussion. I am not, like Catherine Belsey, confident enough in the progressive nature (and importance) of literary study to liken developments in contemporary theory to the "rethinking of cosmology" done by Copernicus, Galileo, Kepler, and Newton, and am more inclined toward Louis Menand's suspicion that "it is absurd to treat literary criticism as a species of scientific inquiry."[5] I wish I could believe that Barthes's work on character advances beyond that of Forster as Werner Heisenberg's work on quantum physics advances beyond that of Neils Bohr, if only because it would provide a more secure sense of the potential value of my own efforts, but I cannot. The impact of contemporary theory on thinking about character has been not to correct but to alter it.

The effects of this alteration have been for me, by and large, positive. Without question, encounters with readers unwilling to entertain seriously the notion that one's subject exists can be frustrating, and repeated efforts to define and contextualize a range of important terms can be exhausting. But ideas always benefit from thoughtful challenge, and postmodern theory has presented a complex, comprehensive challenge to the study of character. Writers about characterization during the past twenty years, myself included, have been forced by developments in theory to make a number of important adjustments:

(1) Whereas character criticism has traditionally attended to the presence (or absence) of similarities between literary characters and human beings, more attention is generally paid now to the *differences* between them, in part as a result of recent arguments that characters are not in fact representations of people, and that language does not in fact represent some other, more "actual" set of objects. A good deal of recent thought has been devoted to the implications of a character's existence within a linguistic structure more limited, ordered, and purposive than the extralinguistic world.

(2) Whereas discussions of characterization have in the past tended to focus on the relations either between characters and authors or, especially, between characters and the people they represent, increased scrutiny is being directed now at the relations between characters and readers: that is, at the role of the reader in determining the effects and effectiveness of character. While this is not a new area of interest— Poe, for instance, distinguished between the realism of a representation and the realism of its *effect*—it is today a more central one. Few

---

5. Catherine Belsey, *Critical Practice*, 145; Louis Menand, "What Are Universities For?" 95.

definitions of "realistic" characterization prior to the last few years took the response of the reader into account.

(3) As in almost every area of literary study, more effort is made now to place the ideas about character at any particular moment within a larger cultural and historical context, and to understand criteria for judging such things as believability and complexity as subject to variation over time. In its most extreme form, this effort has led to the reduction of character itself to a historically circumscribed phenomenon, as when Jonathan Arac writes that "character may be understood as one possible effect of language under certain historical and social conditions."[6] Virtually no theorist today approaches character with the ahistoricity of Forster or Harvey.

In ways that I hope will become clear, Dickens has been a chief beneficiary of this shift in approach, just as he was a chief victim of the Jamesian approach to character dominant in the decades before and after the turn of the century. The weakening of psychological verisimilitude as the central criterion for judging the effectiveness of character, the increased interest in the peculiarities of language, have cast his "highly semiotic, textually-oriented, writerly art" and his "relentless . . . play with the limitations of language" in a most positive light.[7] The challenges to late-nineteenth/early-twentieth-century assumptions about character have created a critical audience receptive to characterization of a different kind. Ironically, the attack on realistic notions of character in general may have led to higher regard for Dickens's characters in particular.

Among the reasons I resist the belief that such developments are progressive is Dickens's perspicacity about his own methods of characterization. Writing a book should provide a few surprises. Perhaps my greatest surprise in writing this one has been the discovery that what Dickens has to say about his own novels within those novels constitutes an astute and complex body of Dickens criticism. To an extent seldom acknowledged, he finds ways within his fiction to highlight, problematize, deconstruct, and parody his own habits as a writer. Recent historical criticism has tended usefully to emphasize the ways writers are moved by social and historical forces beyond

6. Jonathan Arac, "*Hamlet, Little Dorrit,* and the History of Character," 314.
7. James A. Davies, *The Textual Life of Dickens's Characters,* 4; James R. Kincaid, "Viewing and Blurring in Dickens: The Misrepresentation of Representation," 100.

their consciousness or control, and certainly this is true of a writer so enmeshed in his age and so deeply self-divided as Dickens. But I have been struck primarily by the degree to which he seems aware of, if not in control of, his own self-divisions and evasions: not fully aware, of course, but not comfortably oblivious either. It seems difficult at times to say anything *about* Dickens's characters that has not been said *by* those characters or by one of Dickens's narrators—a frustrating situation if one hopes to be original, but a comforting one if one hopes to recover the conditions under which these texts were originally produced.

1

CHARACTERS, CRITICS, CONTRADICTIONS

IN 1965, W. J. Harvey could end his groundbreaking study *Character and the Novel* by remarking on the virtual disappearance of character from the critical discourse of the twentieth century. "Modern criticism, by and large," he notes, "has relegated the treatment of character to the periphery of its attention, has at best given it a polite and perfunctory nod and has regarded it more often as a misguided and misleading abstraction." Not since E. M. Forster's "deceptively light" ruminations on character in *Aspects of the Novel* nearly four decades earlier had there been a signally important or comprehensive examination of the subject; recent discussions had rarely risen above the level of how-to guides for the aspiring novelist. In 1989, by contrast, James Phelan begins his own study of character by citing as influences more than a dozen major works published during the 1970s and 1980s, and his list is neither exhaustive nor inclusive of the many contemporary studies of the characters of individual authors. Where Harvey claims to be filling in a vacuum, Phelan appears to be situating himself within a crowded field of scholars and theorists whose issues and oppositions are clearly defined.[1]

The explosion of interest in character during the last quarter century is somewhat ironic, since it coincides with and probably results from the sustained attack on character as a useful or meaningful critical concept. Scholars of Harvey's generation, or of Forster's, had relatively little to say about the theory of character because there seemed to be relatively few crucial questions to answer or divisive issues to debate. From the point of view of the critic, that is, character appeared not unimportant but uninteresting. Only a handful of critical pronouncements have been as influential—or, perhaps, as representative

---

1. W. J. Harvey, *Character and the Novel*, 192; James Phelan, *Reading People, Reading Plots: Character, Progression, and the Interpretation of Narrative*, 213–14.

of prevailing opinion—as Forster's distinction between flat and round figures, a distinction based on opinions assumed by Forster to be universally held. Of course characters were to be judged on the basis of their resemblance to people, and of course round or lifelike characters were greater achievements than flat or simplified ones.[2] During the middle third of this century, critics spent plenty of time evaluating individual characters but comparatively little time reflecting on the criteria for evaluation. The New Critical emphasis on structure and style (not to mention lyric poetry) further discouraged scholars from dwelling too long on characterization.

The primary challenge to traditional beliefs about character has of course been the structuralist and poststructuralist rebellion against the treatment of literature as representation—and thus, inevitably, against the treatment of characters as representations of people. This is not to say that such a treatment went previously unquestioned: Harvey's final appendix is entitled "The Attack on Character" and details the problems posed by the modernists and New Critics to his own concept of mimesis. José Ortega y Gasset, writing at the same time as Forster, insists that "life is one thing, art is another" and that the novel is an autonomous artifact "incompatible with outer reality." These are mere precursors, however, to the theoretical and political arguments of the structuralists, for many of whom character becomes an irrelevant or, worse, a restrictive and reactionary concept. Essentially critics such as Ortega y Gasset and Q. D. Leavis challenge naive approaches to character—what Leavis would presumably call the lowbrow approaches parodied in L. C. Knights's famous essay, "How Many Children Had Lady Macbeth?"[3] Many recent critics challenge all approaches, or identify discussions of character as by definition naive.

Speculation about character today is conditioned by the tendency of contemporary criticism to reflect more comprehensively than ever before on its own assumptions and methodologies. Consider how different Harvey's statement that "Most great novels exist to reveal

2. Though Forster himself is not as hard on flat characters as are some of his disciples, he does "admit that flat people are not in themselves as big achievements as round ones." *Aspects of the Novel*, 72–73.

3. José Ortega y Gasset, *The Dehumanization of Art and Other Essays on Art, Literature, and Culture*, 10, 96; Q. D. Leavis, *Fiction and the Reading Public*, 59–61; L. C. Knights, "How Many Children Had Lady Macbeth?" 624.

and explore character" sounds three decades after it was made: not only does the term "character" provoke a variety of questions, but the modifier "great" is liable to spark arguments about subjectivity and canon formation and the verbs "reveal and explore" uncertainty about what sort of process is being described.[4] From the perspective of recent reader-response criticism, even the notion that novels "exist" has become suspect. What was once safely assumed is now, at the very least, controversial. Just as the literary historian can no longer operate without some awareness of the distinction between old and new history, so the student of character must acknowledge the differences between the representational and nonrepresentational, or what Phelan calls the "mimetic" and "synthetic," approaches.[5] It might be more accurate, actually, to distinguish among three approaches dominant in this century: the representational, nonrepresentational, and revised representational, each of which has assumed a variety of different forms.

About the representational approach not a great deal need be said, since it is, for most readers, the virtually automatic response to characters in literature. Generally readers assume "full congruity between the way we perceive people in literature and the way we perceive them in life" and tend to judge, interpret, and speculate about individuals in one realm as they would those in the other.[6] Characters, like people, may be interesting or dull, good or evil, handsome or ugly; one may or may not arrive at a satisfactory understanding of their behavior. The best characters, and the most difficult to create, are the ones whose thoughts and actions seem most closely to resemble those of actual human beings, though naturally no character can ever re-create a fully human complexity. With some variation, these assumptions underlie most responses to character in literature prior to the past few decades. A Leavis or Knights may bemoan the tendency to overhumanize the artificial figures of fiction or drama, but, I would argue, their beliefs about character are at bottom not very different from those of the readers they ridicule. They may want to shift the focus of attention from character to language, but not to deny the connections between language and life or the necessity of talking about characters in human terms.

Different indeed from commonplace belief and from the comparatively polite arguments of the New Critics is the blanket, antimimetic

4. Harvey, *Character*, 23.
5. Phelan, *Reading People*, 3.
6. Baruch Hochman, *Character in Literature*, 44.

assertion that characters "can be neither described nor classified in terms of 'persons.' "[7] Adequate summaries exist of the evolution of structural linguistics, formalism, and semiotics into the nonrepresentational theories of structuralism and poststructuralism. Here it will be sufficient to identify the major problems posed by such theories to traditional views of character. In a special 1974 issue of *New Literary History* entitled "Changing Views of Character" that seems to mark the intellectual and historical apogee of the nonrepresentational approach, critics including Fernando Ferrara, Warner Berthoff, and Hélène Cixous challenge mimetic treatments of character as theoretically insupportable and politically disingenuous. Ferrara, in his paradigmatic "Theory and Model for the Structural Analysis of Fiction," asserts that

> This study of character (C) originates from two fundamental postulates: the first states that a character in a narrative fiction fulfills the requirements of all structured systems and is in fact a genetic and transformational structure; the second maintains that the structure of a character is organized at various levels and is divided into deep structure (or genetic matrix), middle structure (or transformational zone) and surface structure (or terminal string).

The nature as much as the content of Ferrara's language points to the shift away from the assumptions of earlier criticism. His models are natural science and linguistics; the structure of characters and the narratives within which they exist can, he posits, be diagrammed as reliably as the structure of a DNA molecule or complex-compound sentence. Like a word in a sentence or a letter in a word, a character derives its significance from the surrounding structure rather than from any reference to an empirically verifiable reality. In this context adjectives such as round and flat, realistic or unrealistic, lose all utility, since they contribute nothing to the understanding of character as a portion of a "structural system." In the terms of such a structural analysis, there is no essential difference between characters and other recurrent elements within a text. Virtually all previous theories of character, even Ortega y Gasset's, had been based at least implicitly on a faith in referentiality that Ferrara's theory abandons.[8]

What is irrelevant for Ferrara is pernicious for Berthoff and Cixous. For such critics, the idea of character is inseparable from the ideology

---

7. Roland Barthes, *Image, Music, Text,* 105.
8. Fernando Ferrara, "Theory and Model for the Structural Analysis of Fiction," 253, 255.

that has largely controlled the production and reception of literature during the past three centuries: a capitalist, bourgeois ideology that remains in power by "controlling the production of the imaginary, by repressing the production of the unconscious that poses a threat to established order." Identification with characters takes place "in the name of some reality principle . . . to which the text is subordinated" and that in turn subordinates the reader to the text, "the reader entering into commerce with the book on condition that he be assured of getting paid back, that is, recompensed by another who is sufficiently similar to or different from him." For Berthoff the term "character" is best rejected as "too much the hostage, with its bias toward individuation, of limited civil and ethical ideologies" and replaced by a consideration of general human properties in literature.[9] Cixous calls for a more radical and politically weighted rejection of the very idea of character:

> So long as we do not put aside "character" and everything it implies in terms of illusion and complicity with classical reasoning and the appropriating economy that such reasoning supports, we will remain locked up in the treadmill of reproduction. We will find ourselves, automatically, in the syndrome of role-playing. So long as we take to be the representation of a true subject that which is only a mask, so long as we ignore the fact that the "subject" is an effect of the unconscious and that it never stops producing the unconscious—which is unanalyzable, uncharacterizable, we will remain prisoners of the monotonous machination that turns every "character" into a marionette.[10]

Beneath the labored paean to an "unanalyzable, uncharacterizable" unconscious lies a fairly clear train of reasoning: the belief in character implies a belief in representation (or reproduction), which itself implies a restrictive understanding of the relations among text, world, and reader. The text is limited to mirroring a world of which it can only be an incomplete simulacrum, and the reader is committed to "figuring out" a text whose meaning is fixed and knowable. In this light Harvey's statement that "Most great novels exist to reveal and explore character" appears not innocuous but imprisoning.

The disagreement between the more extreme proponents of the representational and nonrepresentational approaches cannot, strictly speaking, be called a debate, any more than an atheist can be said

---

9. Cixous, "Character of 'Character,'" 384–86; Berthoff, "'Means,'" 322.
10. Cixous, "Character of 'Character,'" 387.

to be debating a devout believer. The basic premises upon which each position is founded are both unprovable and irreconcilable with those of the opposition: God cannot partially exist, and the writing of literature cannot partially be an act of representation. Nonetheless, the challenges posed by structuralism and poststructuralism have forced mimetic critics to refine their position into what I am calling the revised representational approach to character. In one way or another, theorists such as Seymour Chatman, Martin Price, Baruch Hochman, and Phelan acknowledge the heavy dependence of character on structural context; recognize the immense differences between textual and actual beings; dismiss the notion of judging characters simply in terms of their resemblance to real people; yet remain convinced that, in Price's words, "every element in the novel, from the most abject article or expletive to the most complex character, draws its import and role from some degree of reference to or reminiscence of a world outside." Such criticism attends both to the dissimilarities between text and world—the former obviously "more intensively ordered, more transparently significant, more readily encompassed and studied, more sharply framed and closed" than the latter—and to the habit of characters to inspire, more stubbornly than other literary "structures," speculation that carries the reader beyond the confines of language. The foregrounding of character during the process of reading is neither laudable nor reprehensible, but inevitable. Cixous's reproductive treadmill is for Hochman a necessary path followed and validated by "the critical consensus of virtually all preceding epochs."[11]

That a study such as the present one takes a revised representational approach to character goes almost without saying. The more extreme versions of nonrepresentational theory would deny the very existence of my subject, or would at least look askance at the prospect of devoting an entire book to the discussion of so chimerical an entity as character.[12] Less extreme versions—that is, nonrepresentational theories that grant the existence of character but would discuss it wholly in structural terms—seem, in my view, strained, as if the urge to talk about the relations between characters and people were being kept

---

11. Martin Price, *Forms of Life: Character and Moral Imagination in the Novel,* 55, 43; Hochman, *Character,* 28. See also Seymour Chatman, *Story and Discourse: Narrative Structure in Fiction and Film,* 117–20, and Phelan, *Reading People,* 2.

12. See, for instance, Gass, *Fiction,* 39.

forcibly locked away. If it seems artificial to blur the distinctions between life in language and life in the world, then surely it seems equally
or more so to deny the similarities and to disallow the extratextual
speculation that characters almost invariably inspire. Nonrepresentational theories can do a reasonably good job of explaining, from one
perspective, the interactions between characters and novels, but, in
insisting that what *does* happen during reading should or could not
happen, they do little to clarify the interactions between characters
and readers. Exploring this latter relationship seems to me crucial
for understanding the workings of characters generally and Dickens's
characters particularly.

Having said this, I should emphasize that my sense of representation
as a process and of the criteria according to which it should be
evaluated is very different from what I take to be Forster's or Harvey's.
Representation is not the mirroring of an external world, but the
creation of a world that recalls, partially resembles, and otherwise
relates to a prior one. "The acceptability of a narrative," writes Jerome
Bruner, "obviously cannot depend on its correctly referring to reality,
else there would be no fiction. Realism in fiction must then indeed
be a literary convention rather than a matter of correct reference."
There is no single standard by which all representations should be
judged, certainly not the standard of equivalence to a fixed reality.
Characters that match up point for point with our conception of
actual people are not necessarily the most complex or engaging ones
(if they were, characterization would be a considerably less mysterious
process). To represent appearance or behavior is to establish a more
or less interesting relationship between the textual and extratextual
realms—not to reinforce what we already know about the world,
but to challenge and re-form our knowledge. The most memorable
characters, that is, do not necessarily reproduce recognizable actions
or thoughts, but inspire speculation about the ways people act or think.
"It may be," Bruner adds, "that the plights and the intentional states
depicted in 'successful' fiction sensitize us to experience our own lives
in ways to match,"[13] implying, I think, that the best way to judge
a fictional character may be by considering its effect on the reader,
rather than its correspondence to external reality. A "flat" character
that leads to reflection about the nature of behavior may be more

13. Jerome Bruner, "The Narrative Construction of Reality," 13.

complicated, not to mention more appropriate within a particular fictional context, than a "round" one that resembles our neighbor.

As the best novelists have always realized, moreover, and as critics including George Levine and Philip Weinstein have pointed out, literary representation is also a perpetual struggle to bridge the unbridgeable gap between the linguistic and nonlinguistic realms.[14] In realistic fiction, where the effort to re-create the world is more concerted and painstaking than in any other literary form, the frustrations of that struggle are most apparent. The richest characters, perhaps, are those that most dramatically embody the complexity and desperation of the novelist's attempt to represent people in language, revealing as much through what is absent—through what cannot be captured in words— as through what is present. Rather than confirming our understanding of human nature, such characters remind us of its elusiveness and inscrutability.

Not surprisingly, given Dickens's unparalleled popularity and continuing ability to provoke critical commentary, there exists a vast library of reactions to and judgments of his characters. Virtually every scholar and reviewer who has paid more than passing attention to Dickens during the past two centuries has in fact had something to say about the figures who populate his novels. The nature of this critical response, however, is complex and peculiar, in certain respects unlike the response to the characters of any other important novelist. While Dickens is of course too imposing and influential a figure to be overlooked in any comprehensive study of character, his methods are at the same time too unconventional and idiosyncratic to be encompassed by the most sweeping theories of how characters work. Most models that would anatomize the characters of other major novelists in English simply cannot account for the success of Dickens. As a consequence, many critics have found themselves in the uncomfortable position of claiming that Dickens's characters fail although they appear to succeed, or succeed although they ought to fail. Forster's frustrated sleight of hand is well known: "Those who dislike Dickens," he acknowledges, "have an excellent case. He ought to be bad. He is actually one of our big writers, and his immense

14. See the arguments in George Levine, *The Realistic Imagination: English Fiction from Frankenstein to Lady Chatterley,* and Philip M. Weinstein, *The Semantics of Desire: Changing Models of Identity from Dickens to Joyce.*

success with types suggests that there may be more in flatness than the severer critics admit."[15]

Such frustrations may account for the extreme, occasionally hysterical nature of the critical response to Dickens's characterization and for the tendency to spend a disproportionate amount of time on the unresolvable question of whether or not his characters are any good—not in considering how or by what means they work, but simply in pondering whether they work. Plainly this is not the case, or is much less often the case, in the criticism of George Eliot or James Joyce. Rarely does one encounter in discussions of other novelists contempt as undisguised as Aldous Huxley's ("Mentally drowned and blinded by the sticky overflowings of his heart, Dickens was incapable, when moved, of re-creating, in terms of art, the reality which had moved him . . .") or justifications as impassioned as George Santayana's ("When people say Dickens exaggerates, it seems to me they can have no eyes and no ears"). Rarely does one encounter evasions as transparent as E. D. H. Johnson's: "Much as has been written about Dickens' supreme humorous figures, they resist critical analysis. Like their compeers, the great originals of Shakespearean comedy, they enjoy a free and autonomous life, uncircumscribed by the works in which they appear."[16] Only in recent years, as the definition of representation has become more complicated, has the emphasis shifted away from pitched arguments over verisimilitude, though even now critics often begin with the assumption that Dickens needs to be defended against charges of exaggeration or oversimplification. John Kucich, for instance, rejects the perception that Dickens's characters are "flatter than those of other Victorian writers" as "an illusion" produced by their unorthodox construction, and Robert Higbie dismisses such a perception as a consequence of critical biases.[17]

Attention should be paid to the history of Dickens criticism because, among other things, it demonstrates the instability of the literary convention called realism, especially as it relates to the creation of character. Doubtless this is true of novel-criticism generally; but Dickens

---

15. E. M. Forster, *Aspects*, 71–72.

16. Aldous Huxley, "The Vulgarity of Little Nell," 155; George Santayana, "Dickens," 143; E. D. H. Johnson, *Charles Dickens: An Introduction to His Novels*, 120.

17. John Kucich, *Repression in Victorian Fiction: Charlotte Brontë, George Eliot, and Charles Dickens*, 240; Robert Higbie, *Character and Structure in the English Novel*, 121.

has so consistently challenged the criteria by which realistic fiction has been judged and evaluated, so relentlessly forced critics to be explicit about those criteria, that the history of response to his work, and particularly to his characters, is unusually revealing. His critical reputation at any given moment has been partly, perhaps largely, determined by the model of realistic characterization then in vogue: thus his collapse during the last decades of the nineteenth century and first decades of the twentieth, when a Jamesian model incompatible with Dickens's methods was clearly dominant, and his lionization during the past several years, when the sorts of distortion found in his work have been greeted with toleration or enthusiasm. Few examples more definitively bear out Jerome McGann's observation that "criticism is necessarily tendentious in its operations."[18]

By what standards have characters in realistic fiction customarily been judged? The history of response to Dickens's characters reveals a handful of criteria to be recurrent and, to varying degrees, fluid. Probably the most recurrent and least fluid is the standard of interiority, that is, the expectation that the best characters will be endowed with complex and carefully rendered internal lives. The representation of external life has rarely been paid comparable attention, the assumption presumably being that any reasonably skilled writer can depict a face or form, whereas the representation of psychological and emotional states has been considered the novelist's ultimate test. Because Dickens is more often seen to have failed this test than is any other major novelist, interiority (or its absence) is a persistent theme in the criticism of his work. By the time Henry James calls Dickens, in 1865, "the greatest of superficial novelists," he is already reiterating a familiar judgment, one subsequently echoed in 1934 by David Cecil, who complains that Dickens typically "lost sight of the inner man altogether"; in 1940 by George Orwell, who detects in Dickens's characters "no mental life"; in 1965 by Robert Garis, who cites Dickens's "lack of interest in the inner lives of others"; in 1982 by David Simpson, who acknowledges that "the recitation . . . of the operations of intimately described and deployed mental states . . . is not an option that Dickens's writing seems to mean to permit us"; and so on nearly ad infinitum.[19]

---

18. Jerome J. McGann, *The Beauty of Inflections: Literary Investigations in Historical Method and Theory*, 25.

19. Henry James, *Theory of Fiction*, 213; David Cecil, *Early Victorian Novelists*, 42; George Orwell, *A Collection of Essays*, 99; Robert Garis, *The Dickens*

Until recently, the only important variable in this refrain was whether the critic found the absence of "intimately described . . . mental states" a fatal flaw (as did the young James) or a weakness balanced by other strengths (as did Orwell). The advisability of endowing characters with complex, individualized internal lives was seldom questioned, since the automatic assumption was that the best characters were the most accurate reproductions of people and people did in fact possess such internal lives. Hence contemporary rejections and redefinitions of representation have benefited Dickens's reputation immensely by weakening the hold of the criterion that perhaps weighed most heavily against him. In particular, the inclination among psychoanalysts "to conceive the personality not as an atomistic unit but as a play of complex and competing processes" and among structuralists to dismiss "the uniqueness and singularity of character" has forced even mimetic critics to revise their ideal model of the interesting and effective character, or to cease valorizing a single model.[20] The Jamesian argument remains powerful, but is no longer unchallenged.

Nearly as powerful has been the belief that the best characters "develop" during the course of a novel: not only do they possess inner lives, but those lives alter, or at least reveal themselves to be unexpectedly multifaceted, as the narrative proceeds. Static characters may serve to fill in the background or elaborate on a theme but are, to invoke Forster again, "not in themselves as big achievements" as developing ones.[21] So reflexive is this assessment now that its historicity is easily overlooked. The truth is that the use of change as a criterion for judging character is a relatively recent development related to the sense of history and progress that arose during the nineteenth century and contributed in many ways to the formation of modern thought. "It is only in the nineteenth century," observes Barbara Foley, "that the term 'history' comes to denote not merely a mode of discourse or a universal process of change, but a crucial context for understanding the present."[22] This is so on an individual as well as a social or national

---

Theatre: A Reassessment of the Novels, 61; David Simpson, Fetishism and Imagination: Dickens, Melville, Conrad, 40.

20. Karen Chase, Eros and Psyche: The Representation of Personality in Charlotte Brontë, Charles Dickens, George Eliot, 32; Thomas Docherty, Reading (Absent) Character: Towards a Theory of Characterization in Fiction, xii.

21. E. M. Forster, Aspects, 73.

22. Barbara Foley, Telling the Truth: The Theory and Practice of Documentary Fiction, 144. The most influential exponent of this view has of course been Michel

level, so that, more than ever before, a knowledge of personal history comes to be seen as crucial to the understanding of individuals in the present. And what was true of people was expected to be true of literary characters: the most realistic should have discernible histories, should progress and evolve through time. Precisely the same beliefs that led to the veneration of history as a discipline—called by Thomas Carlyle the "fittest study" of modern times[23]—or the rise of both the historical novel and the bildungsroman, led to the triumph of the aesthetic that placed a premium on changing characters.

Condemnation of Dickens's characters on the basis of their fixity is virtually absent from criticism through the 1860s, when condemnation on other grounds was common enough. Far more prevalent, in fact, is praise for Dickens's ability to embody in changeless form what R. H. Horne calls "universal laws" and John Forster calls "principles of character universal as nature itself." Even James, who in 1865 finds so much to castigate, makes no mention of the failure of Dickens's characters to change. By the 1870s, however, Walter Pater is describing consciousness as "that strange, perpetual weaving and unweaving of ourselves" and critics are beginning to look with disapproval at the relatively static creations of Dickens and other Victorian and pre-Victorian novelists. George Henry Lewes signals an important shift in critical priorities when he complains in 1872 that Dickens's "characters have nothing fluctuating or incalculable about them," viewing as a liability something that most earlier readers would have considered a strength. Modernist methods of characterization foregrounded change, and the privileging of the modernist example made widespread the estimation that the "tacit assumption of Victorian fictionalists is that the actualities of life are not to go into the book." While belief in this damning "tacit assumption" is much less strong today, still it seems fair to say, with John Bayley, that the "modern idea of personality is of a state of flux, in which new attitudes are [constantly] forming,"[24] and still the prevailing belief among mimetic critics appears to be that the

---

Foucault. See *The Order of Things: An Archeology of the Human Sciences*, 217–21.

23. Thomas Carlyle, *Selected Essays*, 91.

24. R. H. Horne, *A New Spirit of the Age*, 17; John Forster, *The Life of Charles Dickens*, 1: 128; Walter Pater, *The Renaissance*, 236; George Henry Lewes, "Dickens in Relation to Criticism," 65–66; Walter L. Myers, *The Later Realism: A Study of Characterization in the British Novel*, 12; John Bayley, *The Characters of Love: A Study in the Literature of Personality*, 286.

most realistic characters represent or re-create such a state. Generally Dickens fares poorly under this model, at least without some rather obvious straining to redefine terms or reconceive characters.

No criterion has been more central or controversial in the response to Dickens's characters than what might be called proportionality. In the view of most critics, the evolving internal lives of the best characters should be unexaggerated, at least if the intention is to be believable. Extreme attitudes, grotesque behavior, and overwhelming emotions produce cartoons and stereotypes, not realistic figures. The importance of this standard explains the intensity of Santayana's defense of Dickens and the attempt of George Bernard Shaw, another passionate advocate, to evade the issue altogether by insisting that "Dickens's business in life has become too serious for troubling over the small change of verisimilitude." More typical is the complaint of William Dean Howells that the "motives [of Dickens's characters] are as disproportioned and improbable, and their passions and purposes as overcharged, as those of the worst of Balzac's people." From the beginning, however, a sizable minority has acknowledged yet applauded Dickens's exaggerated characterization, citing it as appropriate for his purposes or even as the key to his success. While the terms of such analyses are often frustratingly vague—Dickens "did not always manage to make his characters men," G. K. Chesterton admits, "but he always managed, at the least, to make them gods"—the intention clearly is to dismiss proportionality as a universal standard for judging effective characterization. One common strategy is to remove Dickens from the realm, and thus free him from the rules, of realistic fiction: "Dickens's figures belong to poetry," insists T. S. Eliot, "like figures of Dante or Shakespeare," and betray "no process or calculation."[25]

Uncovered by these differences of opinion is one of the crucial ambiguities in the traditional definition of realism: should the realistic character appear lifelike or produce a lifelike response in the reader? Should a fictional murderer mirror the details of an actual one or, in whatever way possible, generate terror and revulsion? These questions are very old ones, and since the middle of the nineteenth century they have been raised more frequently in the criticism of Dickens than in that of any other English novelist. Well before James was

25. George Bernard Shaw, "Hard Times," 131; William Dean Howells, Criticism and Fiction and Other Essays, 82; G. K. Chesterton, "The Pickwick Papers," 114; T. S. Eliot, "Wilkie Collins and Dickens," 152.

negatively reviewing Dickens's grotesqueries, Poe was praising them on the grounds that "we do not paint an object to be true, but to appear true to the beholder." Contemporaneous with Howells's judgment is George Saintsbury's that "although, or because, extravagance is of their essence, we seldom . . . feel [Dickens's characters] to be extravagant." Anthony Trollope appears troubled by precisely this issue when he acknowledges that "Mrs. Gamp, Micawber, Pecksniff, and others have become household words in every house, as though they were human beings; but to my judgment they are not human beings, nor are any of the characters human which Dickens has portrayed. It has been the peculiarity and marvel of this man's power, that he has invested his puppets with a charm that has enabled him to dispense with human nature."[26] What Trollope is really saying, with a mix of annoyance and admiration, is that Dickens's characters do not *resemble* human beings, yet to most readers they *seem* none the less human. Their mimetic accuracy lies in their impact rather than in their convincing mimicry of actual appearance or behavior. He is mystified because he is caught between two conflicting definitions of realism.

Modern critics have been less mystified by, but no more prepared to resolve, the conflict between representation-oriented and reception-oriented theories of character. Indeed, the conflict has grown more stark as mimetic theory and reception theory have become more self-conscious and less compatible. In its more extreme forms, reception theory would dissolve the text itself into a set of cues or starting points and locate the literary experience wholly in the interactions between language and reader. "Reading is not a matter of discovering what the text means," Terry Eagleton summarizes, "but a process of experiencing what it *does* to you." Neither is interpretation a matter of discovering what the text represents: from the perspective of such criticism, terms such as "lifelike" or "exaggerated" only have meaning when applied to the responses of the reader. Thus Thomas Docherty argues that "the meaning of a character is located in our response to or interrelations with the described character. In other words, a literary character is never actually laid open to our dissecting critical sharpness; it is rather the case that descriptions of character establish certain positions or interrelations between character and

---

26. Edgar Allan Poe, *"The Old Curiosity Shop,"* 22; George Saintsbury, *Corrected Impressions: Essays on Victorian Writers,* 133; Anthony Trollope, *Autobiography,* 75.

reader."[27] Many reception theorists would not deny that a character can be stereotypical or intensified, but would make the basis for that judgment the nature of the response produced in the reader rather than the nature of the correspondence between the text and the world.

The valuation of interiority, development, and proportionality is based upon the assumed likeness between characters and human beings; the importance of a fourth standard is based upon the assumed interdependence of characters and the texts they inhabit. Nearly as influential as Forster's definition of flat and round characters have been James's rhetorical questions—"What is character but the determination of incident? What is incident but the illustration of character?"— that are less descriptions of all novels than prescriptions for how novels should ideally be constructed.[28] Beginning in the late nineteenth century, the belief took hold, or at least intensified, that character should always serve a clear purpose in the plot or thematic framework of a novel; characters created merely as free-floating entertainments or embodiments of life were liabilities. Very different is the aesthetic of an earlier novelist like Wilkie Collins, who observes that "It may be possible in novel-writing to present character successfully without telling a story; but it is not possible to tell a story successfully without presenting characters." Collins's view reflects the Romantic prioritization of character that shaped literature and criticism through much of the nineteenth century, whereas James's reflects his own perception of the novel as "a living thing, all one and continuous, like any other organism," in which all components must contribute to the functioning of the whole.[29] The organic metaphor, shifting the literary "life" from the people in the text to the text itself, signals a deemphasis of character and a growing inclination to analyze fiction as one would analyze the most overtly organic literary form, the lyric poem.

The initial effect of this new aesthetic on judgments of Dickens is typified by David Cecil's blanket assertion that Dickens "cannot construct. . . . His books have no organic unity; they are full of characters who serve no purpose in furthering the plot." Note the equation of "organic unity" with plot-subservient characterization. Even friendlier

27. Terry Eagleton, *Literary Theory: An Introduction,* 85; Docherty, *(Absent) Character.*

28. James, *Theory of Fiction,* 36–37.

29. Wilkie Collins, Preface to *The Woman in White,* 2d ed., 32; James, *Theory of Fiction,* 76.

critics such as Gissing and Chesterton are prepared to concede that character and event in Dickens are not intrinsically related.[30] The rise of structuralism, paradoxically, with its greatly strengthened belief in fiction as a closed and interrelated system, actually improved Dickens's standing by altering the organic metaphor from a prescription for good texts to a description of all texts. If all characters are, in Steven Connor's phrase, "the symptoms of structure,"[31] then Dickens's apparent excrescences must be redefined as components whose relations to the whole are less obvious. Thus was launched the ongoing search to discover the structural relevance of even the most apparently inconsequential of Dickens's characters and the transformation of the novelist who could not construct into the brilliant if sometimes unconscious architect evoked in contemporary criticism.

This list of standards is meant not to be exhaustive, but to suggest the historical variability of criteria for judging characters and the tendency of many of the criteria dominant during the past century to weigh against the characters of Dickens. Some critics have accepted the realist model of character and attempted to defend Dickens on its terms, arguing that his characters have richer inner lives or develop more or fit more neatly into his plots than is generally imagined. It seems to me, however, that when judged by such standards as internality and proportionality, Dickens's characters fail as often as they succeed, and that such standards do little to account for the response typically generated by those characters. Certainly many novelists have surpassed Dickens in the creation of characters in the Jamesian or Forsterian mold. Better to accept Dickens's characters on their own terms: to acknowledge, that is, that their internal lives are often less scrupulously represented than their external appearance; that those lives are often static and, from a realistic perspective, exaggerated; and that the relations between character and text are often difficult to discern. Rather than leading to the condemnation of Dickens's characterization, such acknowledgments—really rather obvious—should lead beyond the realist model to a consideration of alternate ways of effectively representing personality.

The special problems posed by Dickens's characters will be used here as starting points for investigations into their nature. Because

---

30. Cecil, *Early Victorian Novelists*, 27; George Gissing, *Charles Dickens*, 109; G. K. Chesterton, *Charles Dickens*, 14–15, 80–82.

31. Steven Connor, *Charles Dickens*, 28.

Dickens places unusual emphasis on external appearance, I explore
the distinguishing qualities of his descriptive language, its effect on the
reader, and the set of attitudes it typically conveys; because he does
in fact populate his novels with many fixed and exaggerated types,
I consider the implications and potential benefits of so unorthodox
a presentation of personality; and because his creations do regularly
challenge the criterion of organic unity, I examine the relations between character and structure in both Dickens particularly and the
novel more generally. What emerges, I think, is a fairly clear sense of
Dickens's response to human behavior and to the problems inherent
in the novelist's attempt to re-create it: as I hope will become evident,
each apparently independent peculiarity of his characterization can
be traced to an imagination troubled by the difficulties of seeing,
judging, and representing people in language. The true marvel is not, as
Trollope believed, that Dickens managed to succeed despite dispensing
with human nature, but that he managed to transform doubt and self-
division into a source of artistic strength.

Among all the changes in the way Dickens has been imagined
and judged, none has been more dramatic than the shift from the
perception of him as an energetically confident and straightforward
novelist—The Inimitable—to the perception of him as a novelist of
doubt, conflict, and contradiction. Prior to the last half century, readers
who admired and reviled Dickens tended at least to share the sense
that he knew what he wanted to say and said it directly: the important
question was whether one found the message brilliant or banal. Partly
this view arose from the public mythologizing of Dickens into a
dynamo who tossed off novels just as he strode through London, at
breakneck speed; partly it resulted from the sheer volume and rapidity
of his early production; partly, and especially after Dickens's death, it
grew from the belief that, as Sean O'Faolain put it, "Dickens was
not in the modern and rather priggish sense an 'artist'" but was
instead a natural talent who happened to write novels.[32] Terms like
"effortless" and "exuberant" are as recurrent in nineteenth- and early-
twentieth-century Dickens criticism as in the premodern criticism of
Shakespeare.

Edmund Wilson's version of a tortured, deeply ambivalent Dickens
began to change all this, though I suspect that Wilson himself would

32. Sean O'Faolain, *The English Novel*, 150.

be shocked by the degree to which Dickens has come to be seen
as self-divided. That perception today is widespread and assumes a
variety of forms. Following Wilson's lead, psychoanalytic critics have
emphasized what John Kucich describes as "the contradiction between
Dickens's delighted identification with violent forms of desire and his
careful repression of desire in his heroes and heroines" or what Gwen
Watkins, more bluntly, describes as the "schizoid aspect of Dickens."[33]
More linguistically or structurally oriented critics have focused on the
"unresolved tension" in Dickens's work and its tendency to reveal
"an internal resistance to its own premises." Others have noted that
"Dickens . . . presents violently contradictory, fiercely battling notions
of what constitutes the self," that he is plagued by "tragic doubt," and
that he is "essentially an uncertain observer."[34] Kate Flint has perhaps
been most emphatic on this point: "Dickens is an author whose writings continually contradict themselves. Moreover, this contradiction
is a pattern which goes far beyond attitudes to specific issues, such as
home or imprisonment, industry or the pastoral. It extends to tone, to
the alternation of optimism and pessimism, comedy and tragedy, to
the variety of voices which are heard within Dickens's novels."[35]

Clearly this understanding of Dickens has much to do with the qualities valorized by contemporary criticism. As different as new criticism
is from new historicism, or psychoanalysis from deconstruction, all
seem to be embraced by practitioners who take their greatest pleasure
in uncovering the conflicts and oppositions woven into the language
and ideas of the literary text. The ironies attended to by new critics,
like the power struggles highlighted by new historicists and the fissures
between language and meaning claimed by deconstructionists, are examples of unresolved tension. Nevertheless, a heightened sensitivity to
contradictory impulses may in this instance be particularly rewarding.
True, Dickens's ambivalence and uncertainty have been foregrounded
recently because criticism has become increasingly interested in such
qualities; but, equally true, Dickens has proved to be so attractive to
contemporary critics because his work is rife with the tensions and

33. Kucich, *Repression*, 201; Gwen Watkins, *Dickens in Search of Himself:
Recurrent Themes and Characters in the Works of Charles Dickens*, 2.
34. Higbie, *Character and Structure*, 126; Weinstein, *Semantics*, 19; James R.
Kincaid, "Performance, Roles, and the Nature of the Self," 12; Chase, *Eros and
Psyche*, 95; James A. Davies, *Textual Life*, 10.
35. Kate Flint, *Dickens*, 39.

contradictions they seek out. The marriage of subject to critical taste seems ideal.

I wish to explore here the specific relations between Dickens's ambivalent or self-contradictory imagination and his creation of character. That a novelist given to interesting forms of doubt should be particularly doubtful when representing people is of course unsurprising, since people (or their fictional analogues) are the most central, complicated, and potentially duplicitous objects in nearly all works of literature. I would go further, however, and argue that contradiction and uncertainty do not merely color Dickens's characterization but account in large part for its distinctiveness and success. Dickens's characters, that is, tend to impress precisely to the extent that they are marked by powerful opposition, or, to put it another way, derive their most interesting energies from the play of unresolved tensions. By a strange paradox, he fails most dramatically when he appears most assured about the nature of a character, though I would add that such assurance is less frequent than is generally imagined. This recognition helps circumvent the question of verisimilitude and redirects attention to the processes through which Dickens's characters are created, the forms they assume, and the effects they have on the reader.

In calling Dickens's creation of character a fundamentally doubtful process, I am pointing not to uncertain or unskilled artistic execution but to a combination of uncertain attitudes: about the possibility of seeing clearly, of discovering the truth through an apprehension of surface images, of understanding human personality, of representing actual people and objects accurately in language. Virtually all biographical evidence suggests that Dickens believed himself to be an extraordinarily gifted observer and recorder of observations. He had few doubts, that is, about his own skills relative to those of other novelists. But his fiction reveals a profound and increasing anxiety about the potential for even the most perceptive observer to see reliably, for even the most fluent recorder to describe meaningfully, and, consequently, for any novelist to do more than struggle fruitlessly to arrive at the truth. Here, perhaps, is the unresolved tension in Dickens's writing that underlies all the others: the brilliant creator, energetic and ambitious, is locked in perpetual conflict with his own doubts about the value and truth of his creations.

Naturally some of Dickens's characters are as simple and straightforward as they appear to be. Often, however, especially in his mature novels, polysemous descriptive prose, divided personalities, images of doubling and inversion, and problematic relations between character and structure create elusive fictional beings. Baruch Hochman has identified the essential difference between Homo Fictus and Homo Sapiens, or people in literature and people in life, as the tendency of the former to appear more "coherent and meaningful" because of the selectivity and structure imposed by textual constraints.[36] It is precisely this appearance of coherence and meaning that Dickens undermines, thereby generating an even fuller congruity between our perception of literary and actual beings. He re-creates the difficulty and indecision with which we apprehend people more than the contours of the people themselves. As Susan Horton has suggested, "The effect on us of this not-completely controlled fictive world is a near-approximation of the richness, the complexity and the bewilderment that is a part of life in the very real world, which, of course, is neither limited nor controlled."[37] The characters of Henry James or James Joyce have traditionally been seen as lifelike on the basis of the elaborate detail in which their internal lives are rendered; yet how often, in life, do we apprehend with Jamesian certainty or Joycean specificity the consciousness or personality of another? More often than not, even those people we know best retain a powerful aura of mystery—an aura shared by the best of Dickens's characters.[38]

No character is without some element of the uncertain or imprecise, if only because no physical or psychological description can ever be exhaustive; many, for better or worse, seem self-contradictory or inconsistent. Dickens, however, carries these ordinary uncertainties and contradictions to extraordinary lengths, preventing confident judgments about the appearance, personality, and novelistic purpose of many of his characters. Typically he does this through some combination of the following procedures:

(1) By incorporating into his descriptive prose enough qualifications, hesitations, and unresolved conflicts to blur even the most

36. Hochman, *Character,* 62.

37. Susan R. Horton, *The Reader in the Dickens World: Style and Response,* 10.

38. At least part of my argument, I should acknowledge, was anticipated by John Forster as early as 1853. In an unsigned review of *Bleak House,* Forster wrote, "They know little how much there is in one man's head or heart, who expect to have every character in a tale laid before them as on a psychological dissecting table, and demonstrated minutely. We see nobody minutely in real life." Quoted in Philip Collins, ed., *Dickens: The Critical Heritage,* 292.

lengthy and detailed portraits. This is among the most overlooked aspects of Dickens's art, largely because the sheer abundance and particularity of his descriptions create an impression of precision and assurance. Dickens himself likened his mind to "a sort of capitally prepared and highly sensitive photographic plate," and the nature of early criticism is suggested by Richard Holt Hutton's claim that "all that could be known by the help of astounding capacity for swift, sudden, and keen vision . . . within the field of view at any one moment, Dickens knew and painted."[39] While tempered by the recognition of the selectivity and subjectivity of all representations, these assessments have rarely been seriously challenged. In actuality Dickens's lengthiest and most complex descriptions often raise more questions about appearance and its implications than they answer.

(2) By fragmenting internal lives into differing, even opposed sections that are never subsumed within a single, definable personality. Some characters are themselves collections of irreconcilable fragments, while others are pieces in a larger, self-contradictory whole. Most readers are, as Karen Chase notes, "eager to regard fictional characters as stable entities . . . [with] fixed bounds, defined attributes, [and] a determinate history."[40] Dickens's fragmentation of personality sometimes frustrates this desire and, consequently, the ordinary strategies for interpreting and judging character.

(3) By expressing character through images of doubleness, inversion, and opposition such as twins, shadows, and mirrors. Many critics have noted the proliferation of such images in both individual novels and Dickens's fiction generally. Unlike Susan K. Gillman and Robert L. Patten, however, who assert that "Dickens explores the ramifications of doubleness from a base that seems confident about individual identity,"[41] I would argue that the double image usually embodies a profound doubt about the coherence and stability of personality. Often these images lend physical form and increased power to previously expressed uncertainties and contradictions.

(4) By generating a tension between the role a particular character seems designed to play in a novel and some deeper purpose that

39. Richard Lettis, *Dickens on Literature: A Continuing Study of His Aesthetic*, 207; Richard Holt Hutton, *Criticisms on Contemporary Thought and Thinkers: Selections from* The Spectator, 89.

40. Chase, *Eros and Psyche*, 32.

41. Susan K. Gillman and Robert L. Patten, "Dickens: Doubles:: Twain: Twins," 441.

character appears to serve—or even between apparent purpose and purposelessness. This is more than simply the shoddy construction alluded to by Cecil. More than any other Victorian writer, Dickens seems consciously to instigate and then frustrate the search for structural relevance, and thereby to highlight the tension between autonomy and dependence that is so interesting to modern novelists and critics. The attempt to make sense of a character is thwarted not only by the indeterminacy of the character itself but also by the ambiguity of its role within the surrounding narrative.

Enough Dickens figures are shaped by some combination of these practices, especially in his mature novels, to create a pervasive sense that character in this fictional universe is peculiarly complex and elusive. The usual assurance that one can grasp textual beings more fully than actual ones is substantially undermined.

Let me repeat, the contradictions in Dickens's characterization are noteworthy more for their degree than for their mere presence. As deconstruction has shown, language of all kinds is riddled with unresolved tensions; as most psychological models have suggested, consciousness itself is founded on a group of finely balanced (or unbalanced) oppositions; and as recent theories of realism have argued, the limits of the form are perpetually being tested by the vastness of the material. One might contend, in fact, that the self-contradictory nature of the novel has become one of the dominant motifs in recent criticism of the form. Michael McKeon has argued that the novel was at its inception riddled with formal and philosophical tensions, calling it "a contradictory amalgam of inconsistent elements." Lennard Davis locates in the earliest novels the contradictory demands that the reader both suspend disbelief and recognize the fictionality of the text. And D. A. Miller finds a disruption in the tendency of the nineteenth-century novel simultaneously to "censur[e] policing power" and to reinvent it "in *the very practice of novelistic representation.*"[42] Even in this context, however, the linguistic, psychological, and structural contradictions in Dickens's fiction are exceptionally stark and widespread, and the narrative seems to linger over them with unusual self-consciousness. His incessant concern with two problems—how to understand human beings and how to

---

42. See Michael McKeon, *The Origins of the English Novel 1600–1740*, 21; Lennard J. Davis, *Factual Fictions: The Origins of the English Novel*, 23; D. A. Miller, *The Novel and the Police*, 20.

represent such beings reliably in language—shapes, down to the very deepest level, his presentation of character. The "inconsistencies, anxieties, and contradictions" attributed by the narrator of *Little Dorrit* to Arthur Clennam, like the "contest going on within his breast" (*LD*, 403) might be attributed as well to many of Dickens's most memorable figures—and to their creator.

Attending to the contradictions in Dickens should recall, or allow for a new understanding of, his status as an important representative of his age. The paradoxes and oppositions of Victorian culture have been the subject of discussion for decades, and one of the seminal modern studies of that culture—Walter Houghton's *Victorian Frame-of-Mind*—is indeed organized around a set of unresolved tensions.[43] More recently John Lucas has pointed out that Dickens's social criticism is filled with contradictions because his "society is itself one of contradictions, the age is defined by conflicting values, ideas, actualities; and the artist who confronts it is bound to register the fact." And Kate Flint has suggested that ideological uncertainty "was not just peculiar to Dickens, but was representative of far more wide-reaching trends among members of a concerned, questioning, yet apprehensive Victorian middle class."[44] I would further identify contradiction as characteristic of not merely Dickens's attitudes toward society but also his typical ways of seeing and imagining. In truth, he may have been less uncertain about matters of social policy than about more fundamental issues of human appearance and conduct. Like the anxiety of "Dover Beach," his doubtfulness defines a particular moment in history, though Dickens's uncertainty may run even deeper, may be less open to rational reflection, than Arnold's.

Clearly my emphasis on the unresolved tensions in Dickens and on the effects of his characters on the reader needs to be situated in relation to deconstruction and reception theory, with both of which it has some affinity. Like deconstructionists in general, I attend to the linguistic, ideological, and psychological contradictions embedded in Dickens's fiction and to the impossibility of resolving those contradictions into an unequivocal meaning or message. Even his

43. See Walter Houghton, *The Victorian Frame-of-Mind 1830–1870*. Houghton works with such fundamentally opposed pairs as optimism/anxiety and rigidity/openness.

44. John Lucas, *The Melancholy Man: A Study of Dickens's Novels*, 348; Flint, *Dickens*, 111.

apparently precise descriptive language, I argue, dissolves into figures impossible to visualize. But the deconstructive challenge to the referentiality of language is incompatible with my approach here. Moreover, as Jonathan Culler has pointed out, an important aspect of deconstruction is "a suspicion of critics' willingness to celebrate ambiguity as an aesthetic richness,"[45] and that willingness is everywhere apparent in this study. The difference between deconstructive and earlier procedures is less in the recognition than in the interpretation of contradiction. What previously had been drawn upon as a source of irony and complexity is highlighted by deconstructionists as a sign of instability; what had been the foundation of interpretation becomes the undermining of interpretation. While I acknowledge the presence of some degree of contradiction in all texts and the frequent impossibility of resolution, I also see the proliferation of unresolved oppositions more as a distinctive signature of Dickens than as a manifestation of a universal phenomenon. The layering of tensions makes him not typical but peculiar among novelists, and discovery of those tensions leads not to the frustration of interpretation but to the better understanding of the effects of the text on the reader.

Those effects are precisely the concern of the approaches grouped under the headings "reception theory" and "reader-response criticism." To the extent that this book focuses on the reader's reaction to cues provided by Dickens it might be considered reader-response criticism; certainly I share the belief, summarized by Jane Tompkins, that "literary meaning is a function of the reader's response to a text and cannot be described accurately if that response is left out of account." This seems especially important to bear in mind in discussions of character. Unlike the more extreme proponents of reception theory, however, I would not declare the reader's activity "to be *identical with* the text and therefore . . . itself the source of all literary value," nor would I "remov[e] the literary text from the center of critical attention and replac[e] it with the reader's cognitive activity."[46] My concern is with the transactions between text and reader and, if anything, I pay especially close attention to textual details in order to understand the reactions they typically elicit. The response to Dickens's

45. Jonathan Culler, *On Deconstruction: Theory and Criticism after Structuralism*, 240.

46. Jane P. Tompkins, "An Introduction to Reader-Response Criticism," xiii, xvi–xviii.

characters is very much a product of the language and strategies he adopts.

One hesitates to propose yet another general theory of characterization when so many have already failed to explain comprehensively a process of apparently infinite variety. Still, the nature of Dickens's characterization suggests that the traditional emphasis on the relations between characters and the people they represent needs at least to be balanced by some attention to the relations, equally complex, between characters and readers. To say that a character represents a complicated personality is not necessarily to say that it catalyzes a complicated response in the reader. The quest for a definition of "realistic" characterization, probably hopeless already, is made more so by attempting to distinguish a realistic or lifelike image from a lifelike reaction. Dickens, it seems to me, is considerably more adept at producing the latter than the former. That is, his characters do not so much re-create actual individuals as re-create the reactions to actual individuals, and particularly the difficulties and dilemmas. His doubts about the potential for understanding others capture a nearly universal uncertainty, and his struggle to make sense of conflicting, unreliable pieces of information mirrors a struggle we undergo daily. Shunning the rounded and definite, he leaves the reader, like many of the figures in his novels, always contending with the elusive and irreconcilable.

2

"IMMESHED IN UNCERTAINTIES"

The Double Life of *Little Dorrit*

> With the single exception of *Little Dorrit* there is not one of
> [Dickens's] numerous stories that has not touches of the master-
> hand and strokes of indisputable genius.
>
> —Unsigned obituary of Dickens,
> published June 11, 1870,
> in the *Saturday Review*

THE DECISION to center a study of Dickens's characters upon *Little Dorrit* raises two obvious questions: why focus primarily on a single novel and why, given the many possibilities, on *Little Dorrit* in particular? To neither question is there a definitive answer. Surely Dickens's characters might fruitfully be studied by looking carefully at all or many of his works, and—if my tendency to extrapolate from the individual to the general is justified—surely any of his major novels might be examined for traces of his characteristic strategies and habits. But given the extent of Dickens's production and the vastness of characterization as a subject, one must set boundaries somewhere, preferably around an area sufficiently small to allow for more than cursory analysis. Emphasizing one particular novel minimizes (though does not eliminate) the arbitrary picking and choosing typical of more comprehensive studies, allows certain figures and passages to serve as touchstones in the discussion, and, especially, lays bare the relations among characters, language, and structure within a single long fiction. Both the typicality of *Little Dorrit* and the changes through time in Dickens's methods will be clarified periodically by examples drawn from other novels.

The selection of *Little Dorrit* was in truth surprisingly easy. The doubts and inconsistencies typical of Dickens's imagination, as well as the stylistic and structural habits in which they result, all become increasingly apparent as his career progresses. Virtually every attitude and tendency is present, at least in embryo, from the beginning, even beneath the ebullience of *Sketches by Boz* and *The Pickwick Papers*. Indeed, an early novel such as *Oliver Twist* may be more profoundly self-contradictory than many later ones.[1] But for the most part the trend is toward more radical fissures and uncertainties. As Dickens's overt views come more closely to resemble his covert suspicions, or as he grows more prepared to acknowledge the problems undermining his professed beliefs, the role of contradiction in his fiction, and especially in his characterization, becomes more prominent. More characters and scenes convey contradictory messages, and the narrative voice takes up the subject of contradiction itself more directly. This is most true of the long novels—*David Copperfield, Bleak House, Little Dorrit, Great Expectations,* and *Our Mutual Friend*—in which Dickens's characteristic imagination seems most thoroughly engaged. When there is a secondary agenda, such as the anti-utilitarian polemic of *Hard Times* or the Carlylean presentation of history in *A Tale of Two Cities,* Dickens's own voice is more muted.

Little Dorrit, composed and published serially from 1855 to 1857, sits at the center of Dickens's mature period and manifests as clearly as any novel signs of his contradictory imagination. While widely recognized today as a major work, it was viewed for many years as a relative failure and still receives less attention than his other long novels of the 1850s. For many critics of the nineteenth century, Philip Collins remarks, "*Little Dorrit* became a by-word for the bad Dickens," and some of the most notable of Dickens's bad reviews were directed at the book (though these had little effect on its sales, which were excellent).[2] A. W. Ward recalled in 1882 "the general consciousness [during its publication] that *Little Dorrit* was proving unequal to the high-strung expectations which a new work by Dickens then excited in his admirers both young and old,"[3] a feeling generated not merely by the novel's gloominess, but by the perceived inadequacies of its plotting, characterization, and political satire. Even among critics who regretted generally the evolution of Dickens the

---

1. See my article "The Language of Doubt in *Oliver Twist.*"

2. Collins, ed., *Critical Heritage,* 356. For a particularly scathing example of a negative review, see James Fitzjames Stephen, "The License of Modern Novelists," originally published in the *Edinburgh Review* in July 1857 and reprinted in Stephen Wall, ed., *Charles Dickens: A Critical Anthology.*

3. A. W. Ward, *Dickens,* 139.

comic genius into Dickens the mordant social critic, *Little Dorrit* was singled out for special censure: reviews of *Bleak House,* Collins notes, could not match "the severity of the onslaught on *Little Dorrit,*" and the reception of *Our Mutual Friend* was also by comparison "fairly cordial," possibly because reviewers had grown accustomed by then to the darker version of Dickens.[4]

The irony of the early response to *Little Dorrit* lies in the reviewers' tendency to harp on the disorder, carelessness, and signs of depleted power in what was arguably, to that point, Dickens's most carefully planned and executed novel. During its genesis Dickens kept, for the first time, a working notebook, and when its initial number appeared on December 1, 1855, he had, uncharacteristically, three or four subsequent numbers in reserve.[5] His notes for the novel suggest that despite some momentous changes along the way (such as the decision to make William Dorrit a wealthy man), many of the story's most important events, themes, and images were in Dickens's mind from the start. The one criticism that prompted him to make a public response was James Fitzjames Stephen's charge that "the catastrophe in *Little Dorrit,* is evidently borrowed from the recent fall of houses in Tottenham Court Road, which happens to have appeared in the newspapers at a convenient period." Dickens's rejoinder, that "any man accustomed to the critical examination of a book cannot fail, attentively turning over the pages of *Little Dorrit,* to observe that that catastrophe is carefully prepared for from the very first presentation of the old house in the story," is borne out by both the text itself and his working notes.[6]

Despite such planning, and by any measure one uses to establish the popularity of a work, *Little Dorrit* has remained for more than a century the least popular of Dickens's major novels, attracting less critical interest, inspiring fewer adaptations, and adding fewer figures to the popular imagination than most of his other books. In 1953 Lionel Trilling called it "the least established with modern readers" of

4. Collins, ed., *Critical Heritage,* 272, 453. Sylvia Manning has recently noted "two kinds of outrage" in contemporary reviews of *Little Dorrit:* "at the narrator's satire . . . and at the contraventions of form." See "Social Criticism and Textual Subversion in *Little Dorrit,*" 128.

5. See Fred Kaplan, *Dickens: A Biography,* 335, 340.

6. Stephen's remark is in Wall, *Anthology,* 107; Dickens's response, in a piece entitled "Curious Misprint in the Edinburgh Review," appeared originally in *Household Words* on August 1, 1857, and is reprinted in Wall, 114.

Dickens's great novels, adding that it "seems to have retired to the background and shadow of our consciousness of Dickens." Much more recently David Paroissien has noted that "Dickens' two last panoramic novels [*Little Dorrit* and *Our Mutual Friend*] attract fewer writers than one might expect."[7] While no work by Dickens, however minor, can today be described as overlooked, it remains true that *Little Dorrit* has attracted less regular and interesting critical attention than *David Copperfield, Bleak House, Great Expectations,* and even *Our Mutual Friend.* Virtually every recent bibliography of Dickens criticism includes fewer entries for *Little Dorrit* than for those other works, in many cases by a substantial margin.[8] This situation alone, to be honest, is enough to make the novel an attractive subject for a study of the present kind.

Interestingly, this tradition of avoidance has been balanced in recent years by a small but influential chorus of extravagant praise that can probably be traced to Trilling's description of *Little Dorrit* as "one of the most profound of Dickens's novels and one of the most significant works of the nineteenth century." Trilling's crucial move was to insist on the peculiar modernity of the novel, its "relevan[ce] to our sense of things," arising from its treatment of "society in relation to the individual human will" (an assessment subsequently challenged by a number of critics).[9] Later F. R. Leavis called *Little Dorrit* "one of the very greatest of novels" whose "omission from any brief list

7. Lionel Trilling, Introduction to *Little Dorrit,* v; David Paroissien, "Recent Dickens Studies: 1986," 356.

8. For example, in Joseph Gold, *The Stature of Dickens: A Centenary Bibliography,* there are 129 entries for *Bleak House,* 125 for *Great Expectations,* 62 for *Our Mutual Friend,* and 52 for *Little Dorrit;* John J. Fenstermaker, in *Charles Dickens, 1940–1975: An Analytical Subject Index to Periodical Criticism of the Novels and Christmas Books,* includes 162 entries for *Bleak House,* 127 for *Great Expectations,* and 78 each for *Little Dorrit* and *Our Mutual Friend;* and, from 1970 to 1989, the *MLA International Bibliography* includes 192 entries for *Bleak House,* 140 for *Great Expectations,* and (rather coincidentally) 78 each for *Little Dorrit* and *Our Mutual Friend.*

There may be some evidence that very recently interest in *Little Dorrit* has been on the increase—the 1993 edition of *Dickens Studies Annual,* for instance, includes more essays on the novel than on any other—but still the *MLA International Bibliography* from 1990 to 1993 lists far fewer entries on *Little Dorrit* (15) than on *Bleak House* (49) or *Great Expectations* (29).

9. Trilling, Introduction, v–vi. For challenges to Trilling's assessment, see Robert Garis, *The Dickens Theatre: A Reassessment of the Novels,* 181–88, and John Lucas, *The Melancholy Man: A Study of Dickens's Novels,* 251–53.

of the great European novels would be critically indefensible"; and John Lucas, going furthest of all, judged it "Dickens's greatest novel, and far and away the greatest novel in the language."[10] While the extremity of such praise can be explained in part as the defense of an underappreciated work, still it remains remarkable for its degree: *Little Dorrit* is exalted not merely among Dickens's novels, but among "works of the nineteenth century," "European novels," and "novel[s] in the language." By comparison, Michael Squires's recent claim that it is "Dickens's most satisfying novel" seems positively tame.[11]

Both the unpopularity and the effusive, perhaps hyperbolic praise of *Little Dorrit* are attributable, I believe, to the same set of factors. The novel may be the Dickensian equivalent of a Shakespearean problem play, a work that raises difficult questions about intention, form, classification, and a host of other things. As critics have recognized from the start, its protagonists are by any standards, and especially by Dickens's own, unconventional, Clennam in particular bearing little resemblance to Dickens's previous heroes. Its moral categories are not defined with Dickens's usual clarity, its dominant themes are riddled with unresolved tensions, and its shifts in tone can be disorienting. Moreover, the novel takes up psychological, emotional, and ethical issues of extraordinary complexity. "The profundity and complexity of *Little Dorrit* is such," Grahame Smith writes, "that it does not easily yield the depth of its meaning. . . . [T]he difficulty of uncovering a final core of unifying truth seems immense." Robert Garis observes that "to read *Little Dorrit* is to realize that some surprisingly complex and ambiguous things can take place in the Dickens theatre. The old consistent clarities of approval and disapproval have in this novel disappeared: we meet characters about whom it is difficult to make up our minds, and these characters are facing situations correspondingly ambiguous."[12] Among the ambiguities most troubling (or intriguing) to critics have been the inconsistencies in the novel's social criticism ("The attempt to reconcile moral imperatives with social judgment

10. F. R. Leavis and Q. D. Leavis, *Dickens the Novelist,* 213; Lucas, *Melancholy Man,* 251. John Wain, also writing during this period, calls *Little Dorrit* "one of the greatest novels of the nineteenth century" and "the most satisfying of [Dickens's] books." See *"Little Dorrit,"* 175, 186.

11. Michael Squires, "The Structure of Dickens's Imagination in *Little Dorrit,"* 49.

12. Grahame Smith, *Dickens, Money, and Society,* 154; Garis, *Dickens Theatre,* 164.

is one of the sources of tension in the novel, a tension which is left unresolved at the conclusion"); the indeterminacy of its genre ("Beneath the dominant text of the novel . . . runs a set of assumptions quietly subversive of conventional autobiography"); the looseness of the whole Clennam plot ("Given the plot that Dickens is committed to, and his apparent uncertainty . . . , it is understandably difficult for him to write sensible dialogue for his hero"); and the mixed tone of the ending, in some ways more bittersweet than either ending to *Great Expectations*.[13]

One of the few attempts to re-create *Little Dorrit* in another medium merely confirms the novel's elusiveness. Christine Edzard's 1988 film, nearly seven hours long and crammed with period details, is among the lengthiest and most thoughtful screen versions of a Dickens work. And remarkably Edzard manages to preserve some of the original's unresolved tensions by showing many of the same events from two distinctly different perspectives. To make a visually and thematically coherent film, however, Edzard has had to level off many of the novel's more dramatic shifts in tone and intention, transforming Dickens's complex mixture into a fairly straightforward example of social realism. Rigaud is gone, as are many of the novel's more melodramatic and improbable events. Eccentric characters are either eliminated or, through script and performance, normalized. As several reviewers pointed out, the political satire is largely sacrificed in the attempt to focus on the emotional and psychological struggles of Clennam and Little Dorrit.[14] One is left both admiring the film's fidelity to the original text and feeling that an equally faithful yet stylistically antithetical film remains to be made.

Depending upon one's perspective, this profoundly ambiguous novel can be perceived as anything from a mess to a triumph of subtlety and sophistication. Thus, unsurprisingly, Garis can conclude that "in *Little Dorrit* Dickens's newly dark and complex view of his world remains an unassimilated malaise [and] is not transmuted into a successful work of art," whereas Lucas can describe as "one of the most remarkable features" of *Little Dorrit* "the degree to which it seems both random *and* well-ordered." Such variation in judgment

13. George Holoch, "Consciousness and Society in *Little Dorrit,*" 339; Nancy Aycock Metz, "The Blighted Tree and the Book of Fate: Female Models of Storytelling in *Little Dorrit,*" 222; Alexander Welsh, *The City of Dickens,* 134.

14. See especially Gary Wills, "Dorrit without Politics."

typifies the response to all problematic works of art and certainly can be expected in the response to a problematic work by Dickens, from whom many readers expect nothing "fluctuating and incalculable."[15] Has he in this instance transcended his usual straightforwardness or lost his usual sureness of touch? On the answer to that question hinges one's estimate of the novel, and the negative reviews, the relative scarcity of critical analyses, and the instances of high praise all testify to the various forms the answer has assumed.

Fundamentally I share Janet Larson's perception that *"Little Dorrit* is [Dickens's] most profoundly divided novel, formed of many contradictions left largely unresolved,"[16] and therefore consider it especially suited to an exploration of the profound divisions shaping his characterization. It represents one of those moments in Dickens's career when the intractability of his material causes his inconsistencies to be unusually concentrated and sharply defined. The other comparable example is *Oliver Twist,* unique among Dickens's early works for the extent of its contradictions and uncertainties. In that novel we are asked to believe that the "very sage, deep, philosophical men" on the "board" are guilty of abusing the poor while the Brownlows and Maylies are not (*OT,* 11); that Nancy is shaped by her depraved environment but Oliver is ethically and psychologically unscathed; that Mr. Limbkins's reduction of Oliver to a moral example is inhumane but Mr. Brownlow's similar reduction of Fagin is instructive. The difficulty, most readers have sensed, originates in Dickens's inability to make up his mind about the thieves, to resolve the opposition between his sympathy for and identification with civilization's outcasts on the one hand, and his need to validate the moral and social codes of the middle class on the other. What results, according to William Lankford, is a long series of "rhetorical and moral equivocations" affecting the style, structure, and thematic subtext of the novel.[17] The recent death of Mary Hogarth, moreover, may have contributed to a curious hesitancy in the presentation of such innocent figures as Oliver and Rose Maylie.

15. Garis, *Dickens Theatre,* 164; Lucas, *Melancholy Man,* 252; George Henry Lewes, "Dickens in Relation to Criticism," 65–66.

16. Janet L. Larson, *Dickens and the Broken Scripture,* 179. See also Lucas, *Melancholy Man,* 272, where *Little Dorrit* is described as "more questioning, hesitant, and finally far more sombre" than Dickens's earlier novels.

17. William T. Lankford, " 'The Parish Boy's Progress': The Evolving Form of *Oliver Twist,* " 22.

The case of *Little Dorrit* is comparable but more complex. Like *Oliver Twist*, the novel confronts us at every turn with ambiguous and paradoxical situations, but unlike the earlier work, its rifts cannot finally be traced to a single underlying source. Not one central contradiction, but a collection of contradictory attitudes about individual and social responsibility, the potential for freedom, the justifiability of faith, and the meaning of appearances accounts for the novel's difficulties. And whereas *Oliver Twist* struggles, not necessarily successfully, to resolve or deny its self-divisions, *Little Dorrit* appears content, at least by comparison, to present and explore them. Nowhere is this difference more apparent than in the contrast between the novels' endings: in the earlier novel the dark world of Fagin and the thieves is kept safely segregated from the perfect happiness of Oliver's family, while in the later novel the joyous union of Clennam and Little Dorrit is interwoven, literally and thematically, with the "usual uproar" of "the arrogant and the froward and the vain" (*LD*, 826). Interestingly, both novels have been identified as among Dickens's most allegorical—the subtitle of *Oliver Twist* is "The Parish Boy's Progress," and Mildred Newcomb has claimed that "nowhere else in his novels did Dickens so openly declare his allegorical purposes as in *Little Dorrit*"—suggesting that his attempt to abstract general precepts from particular instances may be partially responsible for his uncertainty. If, as Kate Flint suggests, "there was [often] a gap between what Dickens wanted to be true, and what his perceptions told him really was the case," the writing of allegory might prove frustrating: the truths he eventually confronts might be quite different from those he began by intending to reinforce. George Levine, remarking specifically on *Little Dorrit*, makes a similar point: "what Dickens wanted to demonstrate was being confuted by the materials with which, in the spirit of quasi-scientific disinterest, he worked."[18]

No events in Dickens's life contemporaneous with the writing of *Little Dorrit* account obviously for its radical self-divisions—or, to be more accurate, no events reveal why this novel should be any more

---

18. Mildred Newcomb, *The Imagined World of Charles Dickens*, 188. Lucas similarly notes that "*Little Dorrit* has about it the appearance of trying to explore and utter what I have reluctantly to call archetypal truths." *Melancholy Man*, 245. Flint, *Dickens*, 37; George Levine, *Darwin and the Novelists: Patterns of Science in Victorian Fiction*, 164.

self-divided than the others of the 1850s and 1860s. Fred Kaplan calls 1855 a "difficult period" marked by Dickens's painful reencounter with Maria Beadnell, despair at his "lovelessly perfunctory" marriage, and fury at the corruption and incompetence of the British government. In virtually every year from the last third of Dickens's life, however, one can find comparable sources of anxiety, which surely helps explain why his later books are both darker and more equivocal than his earlier ones. Kaplan does note that Dickens's creative habits underwent a significant change just prior to the composition of *Little Dorrit:* "his orderly pattern of anticipating one novel at a time gave way to explosive fragments of alternate possibility, which might or might not be connected, which might or might not become literary realities." Many of these alternate, loosely connected possibilities eventually found their way into the single narrative of *Little Dorrit*. Dickens's letters during this period, additionally, reveal "emotional fragmentation, different parts of himself at war with one another," a condition that undoubtedly carries over into the novel. None of his other works, finally, tries simultaneously for such explicit public satire and such intense, if oblique, self-exploration, different aims that may easily generate structural and thematic tensions. Dickens himself, according to Kaplan, focused with friends on the novel's "satirical dramatization of administrative incompetence" while directing most of his private energies toward plumbing the "dark emanations of his personal life."[19]

If the sources of contradiction in *Little Dorrit* are unclear, the signs are unmistakable. A thorough examination of the novel's many themes is beyond my scope here, but consider, as an example, Trilling's choice as its central subject, "society in relation to the individual human will." The ubiquitous image of the prison, the exhaustive portrait of the Circumlocution Office, and the saga of Mr. Merdle—among many other things—combine to form a scathing attack on the values and practices of mid-Victorian society, with particular emphasis placed on society's tendency to deny freedom, thwart initiative, and corrupt even the best intentions. Yet this angry novel appears at times to internalize and endorse the assumptions of the culture it denounces. Trilling himself recognizes that "it is part of the complexity of this novel which deals so bitterly with society that those of its characters

19. Kaplan, *Dickens,* 329, 335, 342.

who share its social bitterness"—Tattycoram and, especially, Miss Wade—"are by that very fact condemned." George Holoch, writing from a Marxist perspective, has noted that at the end "the moral values the characters have internalized are those explicitly asserted in hypocritical fashion by society": Clennam, Meagles, Pancks, and even Little Dorrit ultimately accept the system of exploitation upon which social action is based. According to Sylvia Manning this is "a text paradoxically enmeshed in the system it is trying to criticize," so that, for instance, "the marriage of Arthur's and Little Dorrit's true minds is as subject to the impediments (and impulses) of cash as are the marriages of Gowan and Pet or Fanny and Edmund Sparkler." Ruth Bernard Yeazell has pointed out "closely juxtaposed" and "apparently unregistered" contradictions in the presentation and judgment of the labor of Daniel Doyce.[20] Every possible response to society, from wholehearted to qualified acceptance, from tentative to utter rejection, is here displayed, found wanting, and challenged by an alternative response. Complicating the novel's social vision still further is its ambivalent view of an underlying moral code—"Duty on Earth; restitution on earth; action on earth" (*LD*, 319)—embraced in various ways by the best and worst of its characters.

Manning has been among the most recent to point out formal contradictions as unresolvable as these ideological ones. "The novel is not seditious," she claims, "because it attacks the Circumlocution Office. If it is seditious at all, it is because it refuses to develop properly. The background plot is close to chaos . . . , the hints about roads of life converging do not pan out, and the ending does not reach closure." Martin Meisel has identified "a paradox in *Little Dorrit*'s agency in that the achievement of a pictorial configuration is linked to the unfreezing of a fixed tableau": the novel tries for pictorial effects yet rejects the truth of the pictorial. Levine, placing Dickens into the broadest of intellectual contexts, notes even that "the strangeness and self-contradictions of the novel enact a conflict between two mythic structures, the progressive vision of Darwinism

20. Trilling, Introduction, vi, xii; Holoch, "Consciousness and Society," 351; Manning, "Social Criticism," 135, 131; Ruth Bernard Yeazell, "Do It or Dorrit," 37. See also Joseph W. Childers, "History, Totality, Opposition: The New Historicism and *Little Dorrit*," 152. "*Little Dorrit*," Childers writes, "finds progress expressed in a number of ways which, when taken together, compose a hodge-podge of often contradictory traits." The new historicism, with its emphasis on competing histories and ideologies, should find fertile ground in *Little Dorrit*.

and the degenerate vision of thermodynamics."[21] In a sense *Little Dorrit* tries (or pretends) to be all things to all novel-readers and ends by being nothing whole: a mystery novel with mysteries unsolved, unintelligible, or unrevealed to those most concerned; a travel novel with almost no travel; a panoramic novel that mistrusts panorama; a multiplot novel whose plots fail to cohere. Clennam never does find out the truth about his personal history, and the connections between the Clennams and the Dorrits, which both Arthur's suspicions and the novel's form imply will be substantial, turn out to be tenuous at best. Since Dickens could be perfectly adept at creating more conventionally satisfying plots, this chaos must be attributed either to a technical breakdown or to a more deliberate attempt by the novel to "subver[t] the conventions of its own form."[22] The history of *Little Dorrit*'s composition, again, suggests no absence of planning, and the presence of so many related contradictions suggests that the unfulfilled plots are, at the very least, more than merely signs of an author unable to construct a story.

Such self-division represents not a loss of artistic control, but complexity born of ambivalence and the refusal to compromise; *Little Dorrit* is less muddied than enriched by its presence. The novel is more willing to recognize social, philosophical, and formal problems than to provide unambiguous solutions, as its somber/celebratory ending makes clear. Manning's claim that "the novel's subversions of plot are probably not conscious" is, like most such claims, unprovable one way or the other.[23] That Dickens was on some level aware of *Little Dorrit*'s unresolved tensions, however, is suggested by the novel's imagery and by its self-conscious wrestling with the nature of contradiction itself. Its opening chapter, even its opening paragraphs, introduce a cluster of related images and metaphors that may be more recurrent and meaningful than the much-discussed image of the prison and that signal Dickens's heightened emphasis on conflict and uncertainty:

Thirty years ago, Marseilles lay burning in the sun, one day.

A blazing sun upon a fierce August day was no greater rarity in southern France then, than at any other time, before or since. Everything in

---

21. Manning, "Social Criticism," 138; Martin Meisel, *Realizations: Narrative, Pictorial, and Theatrical Arts in Nineteenth-Century England*, 315; Levine, *Darwin*, 156.

22. Manning, "Social Criticism," 141.

23. Ibid., 145.

Marseilles, and about Marseilles, had stared at the fervid sky, and been stared at in return, until a staring habit had become universal there. Strangers were stared out of countenance by staring white houses, staring white walls, staring white streets, staring tracts of arid road, staring hills from which verdure was burnt away. The only things to be seen not fixedly staring and glaring were the vines drooping under their load of grapes. These did occasionally wink a little, as the hot air barely moved their faint leaves. (*LD*, 1)

The chapter is entitled "Sun and Shadow," an opposition that marks nearly every environment in the novel and carries through to the "sunshine and shade" of its closing sentence (*LD*, 826). More than simply a complementary pairing, the terms come to invert, mirror, and parallel one another in complicated ways: here, blazing sunshine brings not merely light but, as James Kincaid has pointed out, the threat of "universal blindness," and shadow provides both concealment for the guilty and safety for the innocent.[24] Sweating men "tak[e] refuge" in the shade (*LD*, 1), while prisoners yearn to escape it. The sense of simultaneous opposition and union is reinforced in the next paragraph, where the "foul" harbor is joined and contrasted with the "beautiful" sea, and "the line of demarcation between the two colours, black and blue, showed the point which the pure sea would not pass" (*LD*, 1).

Elaine Showalter and J. Hillis Miller, among others, have noted the centrality of the shadow image in *Little Dorrit*, though without necessarily appreciating its full importance.[25] Above all else, it emerges as the clearest physical manifestation of Dickens's special concern with contradiction and the problems of seeing and understanding. Virtually every setting in the novel, from the Marshalsea to Casby's house to Bleeding Heart Yard, is cloaked in suffocating darkness, and typically the darkness is associated directly with perceptual and conceptual difficulties—particularly for Arthur Clennam, who is disoriented by the "mental confusion and physical darkness" of Tite Barnacle's home at "the blind end of Mews Street" (*LD*, 109–10); frustrated at Miss Wade's, where "the confined entrance was so dark, that it was

24. See Natalie McKnight, *Idiots, Madmen, and Other Prisoners in Dickens,* 112–14. "Dickens," McKnight writes, "uses the sun (and light in general) as an image of surveillance, and contrasts these images with the shadows of the prison" (112). See also Kincaid, "Viewing and Blurring," 103.

25. See Elaine Showalter, "Guilt, Authority, and the Shadows of *Little Dorrit,*" and J. Hillis Miller, *Charles Dickens: The World of His Novels,* 229–30.

impossible to make out distinctly what kind of person opened the door" (*LD*, 326); and, repeatedly, overwhelmed at his mother's by the "premature and preternatural darkness" (*LD*, 344). Many characters, good and bad, emerge from and melt back into shadowy corners: in books 1 and 2, Little Dorrit is glimpsed initially "almost hidden in [a] dark corner" (*LD*, 40) and "silently attentive in her dark corner" (*LD*, 442), and both Flintwinch and Pancks are, in their own ways, forever lingering and listening among the shadows. Like the fog in *Bleak House*, the shadows in *Little Dorrit* are the most obvious environmental constant, though without the bright interruptions provided by the aptly named Esther Summerson, the darkness is even more unremitting.

Shadows are not simply patches of darkness but representations or simulacra, and in *Little Dorrit* they serve time and again as images of replication, distortion, and opposition. Shadows reproduce originals with doubtful reliability, blurring outlines and eliminating details; moreover, they multiply a single figure into two potentially competing ones. Sometimes individuals in the novel are concealed behind their own shadows, as when, in the ghostly Clennam house, "changing distortions of [Mrs. Clennam] in her wheeled chair, of Mr. Flintwinch with his wry neck, of Mistress Affery coming and going, would be thrown upon the house wall that was over the gateway, and would hover there like shadows from a great magic lantern" (*LD*, 178). Sometimes they are revealed and mocked, as when Rigaud sits "with a monstrous shadow imitating him on the wall and ceiling" (*LD*, 445). The difficulties of perceiving appearance and of connecting it to internal character are stressed by the proliferation of these dark doubles, which simultaneously distort and imitate.

Very quickly in *Little Dorrit* the shadow expands from a literal to a metaphoric image that reinforces again the sense of confusion, blindness, and self-division. Miller suggests that the "universal condition" of the inhabitants of this novel is "to be 'shadowed' by some sadness or blindness or delusion or deliberate choice of the worse rather than the better course"; Showalter that "the shadows function as dramatizations of the repressed self."[26] Most often the narrative alludes to the darkening "shadow of the Marshalsea wall" (*LD*, 254), a powerful

---

26. Miller, *World*, 230; Showalter, "Guilt," 32.

embodiment of the damage inflicted on such characters as Little Dorrit, William Dorrit, and especially Clennam by the imprisonment or denial of desire. But this is far from the only metaphoric use of the image: a faint "shadow of Mr. Merdle's complaint" contaminates the complacency of his family and associates (*LD*, 253–54); the "shadow of a supposed act of injustice" haunts Clennam (*LD*, 319), and Henry Gowan "falls like a shadow" on his "clouded face" (*LD*, 403); Minnie Gowan is blighted by "the trace of the shadow under which she lived" (*LD*, 509); and the "dark shadow" of the Clennam house oppresses the immediate neighborhood (*LD*, 542). Most interesting is the appearance of the shadow in the symbolically autobiographical fairy tale narrated by Little Dorrit to Maggy:

> The Princess was such a wonderful Princess that she had the power of knowing secrets, and she said to the tiny woman, Why do you keep it there? This showed her directly that the Princess knew why she lived all alone by herself spinning at her wheel, and she kneeled down at the Princess's feet, and asked her never to betray her. So, the Princess said, I never will betray you. Let me see it. So, the tiny woman closed the shutter of the cottage window and fastened the door, and trembling from head to foot for fear that any one should suspect her, opened a very secret place, and showed the Princess a shadow. (*LD*, 293)

The shadow is "of Some one who had gone by long before; of Some one who had gone on far away, quite out of reach, never, never to come back" (*LD*, 294)—referring presumably both to the absent Arthur Clennam and to that version of herself that Little Dorrit has forever sacrificed. The chiaroscuro of the novel extends from external to internal landscapes, and "Sun and Shadow" becomes equally descriptive of the environment and the psychological life of the characters who inhabit it. Each carries around a kind of inner Marseilles, some parts exposed to blinding light and others buried in darkness, and the relations between the two may be as disorienting as the movement between bright and blackened spaces.

As dominant at the start as the contrast between sun and shadow is the obsessively recurrent motif of staring: ten times in the opening passage quoted earlier, twenty times in the opening chapter, some version of the word "stare" is used. To this can be added eighteen appearances by some form of "look" over the same span, eleven by some form of "see," and ten by some form of "eyes." Overall there are more than seventy allusions in the chapter to the process of visualization, signaling a concern that scarcely abates over the course of a novel in which "images of surveillance are prevalent throughout the narrative."[27]

Characters are continually staring at others and being stared at in return, sometimes becoming trapped in complex networks of seeing and being seen. Affery stares at Rigaud "not only to her own great uneasiness, but manifestly to his, too; and, through them both, to Mrs. Clennam's and Mr. Flintwinch's. Thus a few ghostly moments supervened, when they were all confusedly staring without knowing why" (*LD*, 354). Later, "as Mrs. Clennam never removed her eyes from Blandois . . . , so Jeremiah never removed his from Arthur. It was as if they had tacitly agreed to take their different provinces" (*LD*, 547–48). The story is filled with spies: both unrepentant ones such as Rigaud, Pancks, Flintwinch, and Affery, and more ambivalent ones such as Clennam, who spies on Miss Wade, Cavalletto, who spies on Rigaud, and even Little Dorrit, who observes silently from the corner as dramatic scenes unfold. Characters are incessantly staring and spying in *Little Dorrit* because they exist in a murky, confusing landscape where seeing is difficult and interpreting nearly impossible. From the opening pages of the novel, Kincaid notes, "One cannot see, . . . inside or out—into or out of."[28] The atmosphere is dark, the internal lives of characters even darker. Seeing is also uncomfortably voyeuristic, since individuals are so often unaware of being watched and the acts witnessed so often unsavory. Even Clennam is seduced into spying and, later, into lying to Miss Wade when he claims to have observed her "by mere accident" (*LD*, 656). Surely Dickens's reservations about his own activities as a novelist are being projected onto the struggles of his characters: he is, after all, the ultimate watcher in the novel, with the most pressing need to be precise and reliable. His frustration at the uncertainty of a world where, as for Clennam, "it [is] impossible to make out distinctly what kind of person" one confronts, no matter how hard or skillfully one looks, is paralleled by this series of visual failures and shapes, in ways I shall explore, his descriptive style.

Little Dorrit's general atmosphere of uncertainty and contradiction is combined with a more specific fascination with the elusiveness of character. Of course all of Dickens's novels explore characters, but this one foregrounds and problematizes the nature of character itself

27. McKnight, *Idiots, Madmen*, 111.
28. Kincaid, "Viewing and Blurring," 104.

as do few of the others. The word "character" is used more often in *Little Dorrit*, I suspect, than in any of Dickens's other works; almost certainly it is used more often in ironic, hesitant, or unreliable ways. Like so much else in the novel, this pattern is initiated in the opening chapter, where four times within a page Rigaud uses the word "character" unreliably. " 'I do not advance it as a merit,' " he declares, " 'to be sensitive and brave, but it is my character.' " " 'Frankness' " is additionally " 'a part of [his] character' " (*LD*, 11). Immediately the question of what character is, of how it should be understood, is raised and complicated. While Rigaud remains the most regular and untrustworthy user of "character" throughout the novel, the word is also used by or about Mr. Meagles, Doyce, Pancks, Mrs. Clennam, Tip Dorrit, Mr. Merdle, Tattycoram, Mrs. General, Fanny Dorrit, and especially William Dorrit, usually with considerable irony or uncertainty. Dorrit's reference to "his character as a gentleman" and "his character as a father" (*LD*, 597) calls into question the significance of each noun he employs, as does Mrs. General's tribute to Fanny's " 'force of character' " (*LD*, 473). Pancks alludes to the "character" of Mrs. Clennam (*LD*, 161), Meagles to the "character" of Miss Wade (*LD*, 24), with some uncertainty in each case about whether the term is meant to be complimentary or neutrally descriptive. In this context the word virtually ceases to possess any coherent or consistent meaning.

Also introduced in chapter 1 is the suggestion that character is frequently or perhaps inevitably self-contradictory. Repeatedly the novel focuses on oppositions between incompatible aspects of appearance, between appearance and what the narrator calls "internal character" (*LD*, 149), or between aspects of internal character. Rigaud enters the novel as a physical paradox, with "a certain air of being a handsome man—which he was not; and a certain air of being a well-bred man—which he was not" (*LD*, 10). Each of his reentries is accompanied by similar equivocations, as when the landlady at the Break of Day is "at one moment thinking within herself that this was a handsome man, at another moment that this was an ill-looking man" (*LD*, 128), or when the normally perspicacious Flintwinch is "speechlessly at a loss to know what [Rigaud] meant" (*LD*, 347). Most of the other doubts and self-contradictions referred to are more internal. Both Edward Dorrit and Clennam are portrayed as irrevocably divided personalities, the former filled with "contradictions, vacillations, inconsistencies" (*LD*, 639) and the latter perplexed by "a contention always waging within" (*LD*, 306) and, like the Father of the Marshalsea, "inconsistencies, anxieties, and contradictions" (*LD*, 403). Physician, whose voyeuristic role resembles the novelist's, is often confronted by "irreconcilable moral contradictions" (*LD*, 702), and Fanny, in a phrase with many ramifications, is "immeshed in her uncertainties" (*LD*, 587).

No wonder then that Lucas identifies "a heavy, almost oppressive brooding quality" in *Little Dorrit*, that Kincaid calls it an anticomic "antithesis of *Pickwick*," and that John Wain judges it "Dickens's most tragic novel."[29] Blighted by internal and external shadows, many of the book's characters fail to make adequate sense of themselves or their world. Nor is there a narrative voice that imposes clarity on this murkiness, since the narrator's language and tone suggest "inconsistencies, anxieties, and contradictions" that rival (or parallel) Clennam's. Jonathan Arac has remarked on Clennam's "Hamlet-like self-consciousness,"[30] and indeed *Little Dorrit* might be thought of as *Hamlet*-like in its preoccupation with indecision, self-doubt, and moral ambiguity (as well as its ability to provoke laughter at the darkest moments). Like *Hamlet*, *Little Dorrit* comments reflexively on the constraints and compromises imposed by its form. Even *Hamlet*'s attention to the subtlest implications of language is shared by Dickens's novel: the Prince's famous distinction between "seems" and "is" is perversely echoed by Mrs. Merdle, who informs her husband, most generously, that " 'Seeming would be quite enough: I ask no more' " (*LD*, 397).

Having made the case for the distinctiveness of *Little Dorrit*, let me say again that it remains, in most ways that matter, of a piece with Dickens's other work. He devises no new techniques here, develops no new stylistic habits, and manifests no major new concerns. *Bleak House* and *Our Mutual Friend* are nearly as shadowy as *Little Dorrit*; *Oliver Twist* and *The Old Curiosity Shop* are marked by thematic contradictions of comparable if not equal complexity; *Barnaby Rudge* is similarly drawn to oppositions and inversions; and all of his fiction shares more or less in the language of uncertainty.[31] James Davies has identified uncertainties even in the narrative voice of *Sketches by Boz*,

29. Lucas, *Melancholy Man*, 246; James R. Kincaid, *Dickens and the Rhetoric of Laughter*, 192; Wain, "*Little Dorrit*," 176.

30. Jonathan Arac, "*Hamlet*, *Little Dorrit*, and the History of Character," 315.

31. For discussions of the contradictions in *The Old Curiosity Shop*, see Flint, *Dickens*, 39–42, and Steven Marcus, *Dickens: From Pickwick to Dombey*, 146; for a discussion of opposition in *Barnaby Rudge*, see my article "Physical Opposition in *Barnaby Rudge*."

and Flint has identified contradictions in Dickens's letters, speeches, and prefaces.[32] Little that Dickens wrote, in fact, especially during the last two decades of his life, bears no sign of self-division.

What is noteworthy in Dickens's eleventh novel is the way his characteristic doubts and conflicts combine to shape the fictional structure on virtually every level, resulting in a book as dark, hesitant, self-conscious, and (consequently) interesting as any he produced. And because *Little Dorrit* is founded on contradiction, even appears at times to celebrate it, the contradictory elements in his characterization are granted unusually free rein. Other novels may include physical descriptions as elaborate and uncertain, personalities as starkly divided, images of doubling as memorable, and structural tensions as persistent, but none blends all of these Dickensian elements so thoroughly as *Little Dorrit* and none, therefore, reveals so clearly Dickens's dualistic imagination at work.[33] Just as the student of Dickens's comedy should probably begin with *Pickwick Papers* or the student of his autobiographical impulses with *David Copperfield,* so the student of his contradictory characterization should probably begin with *Little Dorrit.*

My strategy in each of the chapters that follow is to work outward from a close analysis of a single character in *Little Dorrit* to a comprehensive reading of characterization in the novel and then, in more general terms, to a consideration of Dickens's oeuvre. So a discussion of the peculiar appearance of Maggy, the perpetual ten-year-old, becomes a discussion of physical description in *Little Dorrit,* which in turn becomes a discussion of the development of physical description over the course of Dickens's career. I hope in this manner to do justice both to the achievement of *Little Dorrit* and to the ways it resembles and differs from fourteen other substantial texts. In a sense, then, this book is an exercise in analytical synecdoche, with the part standing in for the whole, an exercise possible only because the immensely varied fabric of Dickens's work is threaded with unmistakable and sometimes surprising consistencies. Not just Fanny, not just *Little Dorrit,* but the whole of his fiction is provocatively "immeshed" in uncertainties.

32. See James A. Davies, *Textual Life,* 10, and Flint, *Dickens,* 43–46.
33. I should acknowledge that, in my view, *The Mystery of Edwin Drood* may equal or even surpass *Little Dorrit* in its degree of self-division. Its incompleteness, however, makes it an exceptional and difficult case. Some of the characteristics of that remarkable if fragmentary novel will be discussed in later chapters.

3

Words without Power

H ABLOT K. BROWNE'S illustrations for *Little Dorrit* have from the start been so widely disparaged that even his family has sought to disown them. According to his son the drawings "have an air of being very sketchy" both because "very little work is put in them" and because "large white spaces [were] left and lines not . . . put close together on account of the method of printing." Nonrelations have been equally critical, if less adamant about the causes for failure. Lynton Lamb remarks that "the story of Dickens and his illustrators is that as his prestige grew, the quality of the illustrations declined," citing primarily the demands created by new and more rapid methods of production; Q. D. Leavis senses the "impoverishment" of Phiz's work for *Little Dorrit*, Jane R. Cohen a "failure of creativity," Michael Steig a "definite . . . falling off," technically and imaginatively, even from his relatively uneven work for *Bleak House*. These and other critics have pointed to Browne's being overworked, to his increasing estrangement from Dickens, even to his contamination by the novel's atmosphere of apathy and imprisonment.[1] Browne's own dissatisfaction may be signaled by his uncharacteristic failure to append his name to a single plate in the novel.[2]

Without denying the plausibility of any of these suppositions, I would suggest that the illustrations for *Little Dorrit* do not succeed because they cannot succeed, that any attempt to translate into visual form so unvisualizable a text is doomed to failure, or at least to creating a sense of disjunction between linguistic and pictorial images. Both Leavis and Cohen have argued that in his late novels Dickens was, in Cohen's words, "verbally fashioning his own illustrations" so that "graphic embellishment was becoming redundant, if

---

1. Edgar Browne, *Phiz and Dickens*, 296–97; Q. D. Leavis, "The Dickens Illustrations: Their Function," *Dickens the Novelist*, 360; Jane R. Cohen, *Charles Dickens and His Original Illustrators*, 117; Michael Steig, *Dickens and Phiz*, 131. See also John R. Harvey, *Victorian Novelists and Their Illustrators*, 160.
2. Cohen, *Original Illustrators*, 117.

not superfluous."[3] His increased facility with descriptive prose, that is, left little for even the skilled illustrator to do. I would put the matter somewhat differently: inasmuch as Dickens's descriptions by this point rely heavily on linguistic effects that are not reproducible in visual terms and that challenge even the potential for clear vision, they have become unsuitable for pictorial accompaniment. Martin Meisel makes a related point, suggesting that *Little Dorrit* reveals "a conscious shift in the relations between word and picture in Dickens' narrative mode" and shows Dickens rejecting "the fixed and material image as the equal partner of his art." This particular novel, Meisel claims, is "a celebration of the triumph of the living word over the dead image, of the narrative current . . . over the arrested configuration, of poetry over paint."[4] While I see this separation of the verbal and visual in less celebratory terms, I share Meisel's judgment that Dickens's work in *Little Dorrit* has become inimical to pictorial representation. In an illustration the possible and uncertain become the actual and certain, alternative viewpoints are resolved into a single perspective, the abstract assumes concrete form, and in the process the implications, if not the general outlines, of the original description are lost. There is no visual equivalent of Dickens's mature descriptive language, especially of the language in which he typically describes character.

Of course many of the differences between the images of Dickens and Phiz are inherent in the differences between verbal and visual forms of representation and would exist between the efforts of any writer and illustrator. "Visual images," observes Alvin Kernan, "don't provide the same kind of truth as words. What they say is not necessarily inferior but it is different. Meaning is much more on the surface, experienced immediately rather than discovered by extended in-depth analysis of the image. The meaning of the visual image is also far less complex, lacking the multiplicity of meanings characteristic of single words and the ironic ambivalence set up between words."[5] While this may be broadly accurate, surely the degree of difference between verbal and visual "truth" may vary dramatically from case to case. Some visual images share much of the complexity and resistance to interpretation associated here with the verbal; some verbal images— those in which the multiplicity of meanings is most diverse and the ambivalences most powerfully felt—seem especially unlike anything

---

3. Ibid., 115; see also Q. D. Leavis, "Dickens Illustrations," 360–63.
4. Meisel, *Realizations,* 303, 321.
5. Alvin Kernan, *The Death of Literature,* 149.

visual. To take a simple example: the essential nature of the statement that a character "had curly hair" can be more easily captured in a visual image than would be the case for the statement that he "seemed to have what might have been curly hair" or that he "had hair as curly as a poodle's." The latter statements call attention to their own linguistic existence by employing qualifications and tropes for which there may be visual alternatives but no direct visual equivalents. Dickens's descriptive language is in this sense especially impervious to visual treatment.

A good case in point is the illustration designed to accompany the long introductory description of Maggy, Little Dorrit's mentally impaired companion:

> She was about eight-and-twenty, with large bones, large features, large feet and hands, large eyes and no hair. Her large eyes were limpid and almost colourless; they seemed to be very little affected by light, and to stand unnaturally still. There was also that attentive listening expression, which is seen in the faces of the blind; but she was not blind, having one tolerably serviceable eye. Her face was not exceedingly ugly, though it was only redeemed from being so by a smile; a good-humoured smile, and pleasant in itself, but rendered pitiable by being constantly there. A great white cap, with a quantity of opaque frilling that was always flapping about, apologised for Maggy's baldness, and made it so very difficult for her old black bonnet to retain its place upon her head, that it held round her neck like a gipsy's baby. A commission of haberdashers could alone have reported what the rest of her poor dress was made of; but it had a strong general resemblance to seaweed, with here and there a gigantic tea-leaf. Her shawl looked particularly like a tea-leaf after a long infusion. (*LD,* 100–101)

This is the longest physical description of character in the novel to be represented pictorially by Phiz, and, despite the criticisms, it seems to me that he does a respectable enough job of reproducing some of Dickens's effects ("Where the narrative permits," Meisel acknowledges, "Browne does his best").[6] The drawing, entitled "Little Mother," is, like many of the illustrations for *Little Dorrit,* framed by the blackness of shadows, walls, and mud.[7] Thus the three figures—Arthur Clennam, Little Dorrit, and Maggy—appear to be surrounded by,

---

6. Meisel, *Realizations,* 320.

7. More than half of Browne's forty illustrations for *Little Dorrit* are extremely dark; eight are so-called dark plate etchings created by Browne, appropriately, for Dickens's later novels and fashioned by a painstaking technique of "adding mechanically ruled, very closely spaced lines to the steel in order to produce a 'tint,' a grayish shading of the plate." Steig, *Dickens and Phiz,* 106.

Little Mother

even radiating light into, a swirling, dark cloud. Maggy herself seems
disproportionately large and as expressionless as a stuffed doll; where
Clennam and Little Dorrit are all straight lines, sharp angles, and neat

ovals, she is irregular and askew. Every detail mentioned specifically by Dickens appears prominently in the plate, including most notably the eyes, the smile, the ornate cap and bonnet, and the shapeless, tea-leafy shawl. Browne even manages to suggest the desired stillness, limpidity, and lack of color by leaving the area directly bordering on Maggy's upper body almost devoid of line and shading (though, if Browne's son is to be believed, this is largely fallout from the method of printing).[8]

Not reproducible in visual terms, however, or at least not in a conventional etching, is a set of interrelated attitudes, assumptions, and questions underlying (and undermining) Dickens's description. Absent from the illustration is the curious hesitancy suggested by "seemed" and "about," as well as the pattern of reversal and qualification as the reader weaves from "but" to "though" to "but" in the middle of the passage. Also absent is the introduction of a second perspective—the commission of haberdashers—that emphasizes the uncertainty of the first. Browne makes a decent stab at the tea-leaf, but can of course do little with the gipsy's baby and the seaweed; besides, what are the odds that any but the occasional reader will actually imagine a tea-leaf when looking at the visual version of Maggy? Even the repetition of "large" in the opening sentence produces an effect quite different from the drawing of an unusually large person. Unlike Browne's portrait, Dickens's is detailed without being clear, the processing of its many particulars made difficult by their tendency to challenge, contradict, and blur one another in a variety of complex ways. What results, here and throughout Dickens's fiction, is an extended effort to describe something that is not finally describable, to see something that cannot finally be seen.

As a number of recent commentators have pointed out, specificity and visual clarity in linguistic description are not merely separable but, in certain respects, incompatible. Susan Horton notes that "objects described in great profusion do not simplify the business of seeing: they complicate it," and Daniel Sheridan observes that the reader of Dickens is liable to be "overwhelmed by the onslaught of information."[9] The greater the number of details presented, the greater the need for the processing of information; the more complex the relations among the

---

8. J. Mahoney, in an illustration for the "Household Edition" of Dickens's works, achieves a similar effect by erasing altogether the outline of Maggy's torso and melting her into the background.

9. Horton, *The Reader*, 93; Daniel Sheridan, "The Unreadable *Dombey*," 145.

details, the more difficult it becomes to assemble them into a coherent whole. Too often in the criticism of Dickens the profusion of particulars has been equated with confidence and certainty on the author's part and clarity on the reader's, an equation probably encouraged by the illustrations accompanying the written text. Walter Bagehot's well-known reaction is typical: "we have heard—we do not know whether correctly or incorrectly—that [Dickens] can go down a crowded street and tell you all that is in it, what each shop was, what the grocer's name was, how many scraps of orange peel there were on the pavement. His works give you exactly the same idea."[10] Such a view is less wrong than misleading, implying that Dickens's descriptions are both abundant and hyperclear in the manner of trompe l'oeil painting. In fact it becomes increasingly difficult to understand a world where one is continually being bombarded by so much data and where, moreover, the significance of the data is neither consistent nor certain. What is lifelike in Dickens's descriptions of appearance is not the clarity of the images but the struggle to make sense of a mass of complicated information and to impose meaning on an elusive external world that may, in the end, have no definite meaning at all.

Had Bagehot been writing a century later, he might have referred, as does Rhonda Flaxman, to the "cinematic" quality of Dickens's descriptive prose. This common way of characterizing Dickens, and indeed the long tradition of re-creating his works in theatrical, cinematic, and even cartoon versions, has doubtless contributed as well to the misreading of his language. "In its naive form," James Kincaid writes, "this 'cinematic' notion suggests that there is a movie right there in the novel: all one has to do is slip a camera into the book, follow the directions in the pages, and let the movie emerge."[11] While, as Kincaid acknowledges, few critics and filmmakers are quite so naive, it remains true that the "cinematic" label and the frequent selection of Dickens's work for cinematic treatment implies, at least, a belief in its essential affinity with visual forms of representation. Too often visual interest and complexity—which are unquestionably present—have been automatically equated with visual clarity—which typically is not.

Maggy tumbles into *Little Dorrit* as a perceptual and interpretive dilemma: an adequate description of her unconventional attire, the

10. Walter Bagehot, "Charles Dickens," 126.

11. Rhonda L. Flaxman, *Victorian Word-Painting and Narrative: Toward the Blending of Genres,* 29; Kincaid, "Viewing and Blurring," 99.

narrator confesses, is beyond the powers of the typical observer, or even of any single observer (a "commission of haberdashers" would be required). Similar confessions of difficulty or uncertainty proliferate throughout the novel, partly though not exclusively as a result of its shadowy environments. "One could hardly see" Miss Wade's face because of "the shadow in which she sat, falling like a gloomy veil across her forehead" (*LD*, 23); Little Dorrit's face too is "not easy to make out" in the "removed corners" where she plies her needle (*LD*, 53). Sometimes a particular feature or item of apparel defies description: Rigaud's hair is of "no definable colour," Frederick Dorrit sports "a confusion of grey hair and rusty stock and buckle," Old Nandy wears a coat "of a colour, and cut, that never was the mode anywhere, at any period" (*LD*, 3, 79, 363). Sometimes the interpretive uncertainty is more pronounced: the "key" to understanding the behavior of Mr. F's Aunt is "wanted," as is the "key to [the] inner knowledge" of Mr. Chivery (*LD*, 151, 298); Clennam "could scarcely understand" the manner of Henry Gowan, nor could any observer the inner life of Mrs. General, since "her mind had never traced its name or any other inscription on her face" (*LD*, 205, 450). Mrs. Clennam's "severe face had no thread of relaxation in it, by which any explorer could have been guided to the gloomy labyrinth of her thoughts" (*LD*, 45). Virtually all the extended descriptions of appearance in the novel are situated within this pervasive atmosphere of doubt.

Exemplified in the description of Maggy is Dickens's habit of qualifying, undermining, or even erasing a particular detail with a subsequent one, a move generally signaled by a conjunction such as "but" or "though": the implication that Maggy may be blind is immediately contradicted ("but"); the acceptability of her appearance is qualified by its utter dependence on her smile ("though"); the pleasantness of the smile is itself undermined by its pitiable fixity ("but"). Two particulars are not clearer than one if the second blurs or challenges the first, and a series of such blurrings and challenges may twist the lens out of focus altogether. Often Dickens's contradictory clauses introduce details of emotional or psychological life that come into conflict with and problematize appearance: John Chivery has "rather weak legs and very weak light hair. . . . But he was great of soul" (*LD*, 211–12). More often they establish a tension between surface details, as with the "handsome . . . but [overly] high" nose of Rigaud or the "handsome, but compressed and even cruel mouth" of Miss Wade (*LD*, 3, 24). On occasion these contradictions simply stand as apparently insoluble problems or mysteries: looking at Mr. Casby, "nobody could have said where the wisdom was, or where the virtue was, or where the benignity was; but they all seemed to be somewhere about him" (*LD*, 147). Mr. Merdle appears to shrink from the presence of Society, "but he was always cultivating it nevertheless" (*LD*, 247). While there is nothing noteworthy about the use of "but," "yet," or "though" in descriptive language, in Dickens the reliance on such conjunctions is unusually heavy and unusually prone to generating conflict.

More often noticed is Dickens's habit of qualifying his descriptive claims by using intransitive verbs such as "seems" and "appears," as when he writes here that Maggy's eyes "seemed to be very little affected by light, and to stand unnaturally still." In reality his exceptionally frequent use of such verbs is part of an even more widespread tendency to employ a range of locutions suggesting possibility or uncertainty: conditionals, analogies in the form of "as if," futurities beginning with auxiliary verbs including "may," "might," "could," and "would," qualifiers such as "about" and "perhaps." Dickens's attachment to such expressions has been noted for some time—J. Hillis Miller, Fred Kaplan, and G. L. Brook were among the earliest to do so—but only recently has it been tied to a general hesitancy in his descriptive voice. Kincaid observes that "we are in Dickens bombarded with a cascade of 'seem's,' 'appear to be's,' and similar qualifiers" that "amounts to a kind of waving toward solidity, an admission of relativity in these matters, an indication that the best we can do amounts to an approximation." Susan Horton, who has done more work with Dickens's uncertain language than anyone else, notices in his fiction a "profusion of forms of expression such as *seems, perhaps, if* and *might have been*" that together conceal "a multitude of evasions in the midst of Dickens's rhetorical stance of certainty."[12] I would add that such expressions are especially concentrated, unsurprisingly, in Dickens's descriptions of human appearance.

At times the use of this tentative language is neither subtle nor unexpected: when Dickens writes that Maggy's eyes "seemed to be very little affected by light," or that Rigaud's hand "would have been unusually white, but for the prison grime" (*LD*, 3), he merely makes

12. Miller, *World*, 152; Fred Kaplan, "The Development of Dickens' Style," 152; G. L. Brook, *The Language of Dickens*, 33; Kincaid, "Viewing and Blurring," 99; Horton, *The Reader*, 9, 12–13.

a straightforward and reliable inference on the basis of appearance.
Very often, however, the use of such language is more complicated,
puzzling, or overwhelming. The statement that Casby "seemed to
teem with benignity," or that Pancks "looked as if he had been in
the coals" (*LD*, 147, 148), suggests that the messages delivered by
appearance may be untrustworthy. The intent of the claim that Little
Dorrit "seemed to [have] a pale transparent face, rich in expression"
(*LD*, 53), is less clear, since, so far as one can tell, she does in fact
have such a face and the narrator might have said so without hesitation. The reliability of the supposition that Mrs. Gowan's "dark-
browed and high-nosed" acquaintance "must have had something
real about her, or she could not have existed" (*LD*, 312), is simply
indeterminate. When language of this kind comes in especially heavy
doses, the effect is to create bewildering, unvisualizable descriptions
that exist in a state of *seeming* rather than *being,* carrying the reader
rapidly from one unrealized possibility to another: Pancks "might not
have been quite in earnest, but that the short, hard, rapid manner in
which he shot out these cinders of principles, as if it were done by
mechanical revolvency, seemed irreconcilable with banter" (*LD*, 160–
61). Daniel Doyce "seemed a little depressed, but . . . [i]f he were a
criminal offender, he must surely be an incorrigible hypocrite; and if
he were no offender, why should Mr. Meagles have collared him in the
Circumlocution Office?" (*LD*, 118).

Futurities, "not statements of fact but actions or events that exist
only as conceptions of the mind—possibilities, potentialities, neces-
sities, wishes,"[13] often introduce alternative points of view into a
description, as in the remark that "a commission of haberdashers
could alone have reported" on Maggy's attire. Even as the reader
is "viewing" a character's appearance, he is being reminded that
appearance is subject to multiple ways of viewing, some of which
may or may not be more reliable than others. In some cases the
alternative viewpoint is used to underscore the unreadability of a
particular surface; hence the regular occurrence of phrases such as "no
one could have told" and "nobody could have said" (*LD*, 79, 147).
In other cases the intended difference between the reader's viewpoint
and the alternative viewpoint is not entirely clear. One wonders what
to make, for instance, of the comment that the potential for anger

13. Paul Roberts, *Understanding Grammar,* 171.

in Miss Wade's face "would have been its peculiar impression upon
most observers" (*LD*, 24): is this meant to suggest that the reader is
unlike "most observers"? If not, why the futurity and the hesitation of
"most"? Similarly, is the "compassionate observer [who] might have
urged" sympathy for Barnacle Jr. (*LD*, 108) meant to be distinguished
from the not-so-compassionate reader? The effect of such passages
is less to present right and wrong ways of seeing than to suggest
that seeing itself is a highly subjective process liable to yield different
interpretations, even different images, to different observers, and that
no perspective, perhaps not even the narrator's, is more complete or
reliable than any other.

Even the simple hesitation over Maggy's age is symptomatic of Dickens's doubtful descriptive posture: she is "about eight-and-twenty,"
Pet Meagles "about twenty," Little Dorrit "probably . . . not less than
two-and-twenty" (*LD*, 16, 52), and so on. Less easy to dismiss as
merely colloquial or informal is the hesitation in the statement that "if
[Mrs. General's] eyes had no expression, it was probably because they
had nothing to express" (*LD*, 450). While the uncertainty about the
ages of Maggy, Pet, and Little Dorrit might be attributed to Clennam—
who is present when each is first described—to whom does one at-
tribute the uncertainty about the meaning of Mrs. General's eyes? And
what, precisely, is this viewer uncertain about: whether her eyes in fact
have no expression? Whether they have nothing to express? Whether
the absence of expression signals an absence of internal life? That
Dickens was aware of the potential for such language to conceal more
than it reveals is suggested in *David Copperfield* when the infatuated
David speculates that the eldest Miss Larkins "perhaps . . . may be
about thirty" (*DC*, 268).

A similar tactic is Dickens's very frequent use of "or" and "nor" to
juxtapose differing or contrasting interpretations of appearance. Often
"or" is simply employed, in the manner of "perhaps" or "about,"
to approximate (Mr. F's Aunt's face seems to be damaged in "two
or three places" [*LD*, 157]). More interesting are the instances in
which the conjunction sits between alternative readings of a character:
Flintwinch "might have been . . . either clerk or servant" (*LD*, 32);
Pancks is "very dingy by nature, or very dirty by art, or a compound
of nature and art" (*LD*, 148); Mrs. Merdle wears a ribbon under her
chin "[e]ither because she had a cold, or because it suited her face"
(*LD*, 238); Miss Wade sits alone because "she avoided the rest, or
was avoided" (*LD*, 23). In the last case especially the very different

alternatives introduce an ambiguity that remains palpable throughout the novel.

Another sort of blurring is achieved, ironically, through the proliferation of ingenious and sometimes elaborate visual images. Dickens's fondness for tropes of various kinds is especially evident in his physical descriptions of character, where he seems perpetually to be searching for alternate images through which to grasp the never quite graspable essence of a face or form. Often these images tend, as Stephen Connor has pointed out, to emphasize a description's "lack of definition" by replacing, distorting, or even erasing the original figure.[14] Sometimes they come in rapid, bewildering succession: within two sentences the description of Maggy calls upon the reader to process the images of the gipsy's baby, seaweed, and tea-leaf. Within a similar space Jeremiah Flintwinch's watch is likened to an anchor, his movements to those of a crab, and his posture to the position of the collapsing Clennam house; subsequently he becomes the hanged man, an image that substitutes on several later occasions for any actual description of his appearance. Comparable substitutions of metaphor for physical presence occur when Pancks becomes the Steamboat, Mrs. Merdle the bosom, her footmen powder, and Lord Stiltstalking the Refrigerator. Such substitutions might be considered the ultimate blurrings in the novel, as description is replaced altogether by images that are not, in any real sense, visualizable. Dickens's resort to metaphor is testimony to both the strengths and limitations of language as a descriptive medium, a reminder that language can go beyond the visual but also that the physical world can never be transferred directly into language. If it could—if Dickens were really Bagehot's roving camera lens—reliance on metaphor would be unnecessary.

To the extent that Dickens's most striking images are more often metaphoric than metonymic and more given to blurring than concretizing, his use of descriptive language might be characterized as "poetic." Indeed, the tendency of figurative language to hinder rather than help visualization has long been noted by critics of lyric poetry, especially since the late nineteenth century, when rigorous study of the psychological and physiological nature of image production began. In his discussion of "The Analysis of a Poem," I. A. Richards complains that "too much importance has always been attached to the sensory

14. Connor, *Charles Dickens,* 52.

qualities of images. . . . An image may lose almost all its sensory nature to the point of becoming scarcely an image at all, a mere skeleton."[15] Doubtless Richards has in mind the sort of simile with which Shelley begins "The Triumph of Life":

> Swift as a spirit hastening to his task
> Of glory and of good, the sun sprang forth
> Rejoicing in his splendour. . . . (11.1–3)

The simile here not only fails to clarify the visual picture but actually blurs it by superimposing an essentially symbolic or psychological image over the physical one; and as such images accumulate, the distinctions between physical and spiritual existence become increasingly uncertain. The similar use of imagery in densely textured prose fiction may be even more disorienting, since here, more than in lyric poetry, the reader expects to encounter details that clarify and concretize. Certainly the influential structuralist argument that realistic fiction works primarily through metonymy and contiguity suggests that Dickens's abrupt metaphoric leaps are at least atypical.[16]

Analogies in the form of "as if" and "as though" may be Dickens's favorite descriptive device, possibly because they combine the uncertainty of the conditional with the peculiar imagistic juxtapositions of metaphor, allowing comparisons simultaneously to be introduced and rendered doubtful. "If [Mrs. General's] countenance and hair had a rather floury appearance, as though from living in some transcendentally genteel Mill, it was rather because she was a chalky creation altogether, than because she mended her complexion with violet powder, or had turned grey" (*LD*, 450): here so many different possibilities are combined, through the use of "if," "as though," "rather . . . than," and "or," that both the actuality of Mrs. General's appearance and its underlying causes are mostly obscured. Often the "as if" locution comes in clusters, as if (to borrow a phrase) Dickens has descended into a wholly hypothetical world from which he cannot or will not escape: Rigaud "looked as if the clouds were hurrying from him, as if the wail of the wind and the shuddering of the grass were directed against him, as if the low mysterious plashing of the water murmured against him, as if the fitful autumn night were disturbed by him" (*LD*, 124).

15. I. A. Richards, *Principles of Literary Criticism*, 119–20.

16. See Roman Jakobson and Morris Halle, *Fundamentals of Language*, 76–82.

Dominating Maggy's appearance, finally, is the unnatural largeness of her bones, features, feet, hands, and eyes. The repetition of the same adjective, adverb, or adjectival phrase is among the more interesting of Dickens's descriptive habits, with an effect that transcends, at least in some instances, the rhetorical excessiveness to which he is often drawn. A half-dozen times in *Little Dorrit* alone, introductory descriptions of characters are marked by such repetition, leading to a blurring or obscuring of individual details and an emphasis on the impact of the whole. The more often one is told of the blackness of Pancks or the cold grayness of Mrs. Clennam, the less noticeable becomes any particular black or cold gray feature; in another instance of more being less, the multiplication of the modifier actually reduces visual clarity. Certainly a detail such as Maggy's "large feet" would have been more memorable had it not been presented in the context of so much general largeness. Interestingly, Dickens is especially fond of heightening through repetition his descriptions of angelic young women (Pet Meagles's eyes are "so large, so soft, so bright" and Little Dorrit is "so little and light, so noiseless and shy, and . . . so conscious of being out of place" [*LD*, 16, 52]), characters who remain, for a variety of reasons, among his least visualizable—even when, as in the case of Little Dorrit, he describes them in two extensive paragraphs.

Sometimes repetition can go beyond obscuring traits and actually challenge or problematize their meaning, as in the description of the "large unfeeling handsome eyes, and dark unfeeling handsome hair, and . . . broad unfeeling handsome bosom" of Mrs. Merdle (*LD*, 238). The repetition of "handsome," along with its linkage to "unfeeling," calls into question the significance of an ordinarily complimentary adjective. The attribution of qualities to inappropriate objects— "unfeeling . . . hair"—makes it clear that the visual particulars here are less important than the general impression. This form of repetition is seen most definitively in *Our Mutual Friend*, where Dickens writes that "Bradley Headstone, in his decent black coat and waistcoat, and decent white shirt, and decent formal black tie, and decent pantaloons of pepper and salt, with his decent silver watch in his pocket and its decent hair-guard round his neck, looked a thoroughly decent young man of six-and-twenty" (*OMF*, 217). By the end of this detailed yet essentially unvisualizable description, Headstone's decency has both obscured all the other specifics of his appearance and come to seem, somehow, frighteningly indecent.

Taken as a whole, these conjunctions, verbs, modifiers, metaphors, and repetitions make the portrait of Maggy a concentrated but representative example of Dickens's descriptive prose. Here and throughout his fiction appear contradictions, uncertainties, multiple perspectives, hints of something unexplained, together creating the picture of visual details engaged in a figurative struggle. This is not in any sense hyperclarity. Rather, it is abundance trying always to clarify what is fundamentally ambiguous and can never be wholly captured. When Dickens combines details a, b, and c, one occasionally gets a+b+c, but more often a+b-c, or a+b and what seems to be c, or a, perhaps b, and in another's opinion c. One finds not the straightforward accretion of physical particulars but repeated attempts to visualize clearly that modify and test the resourcefulness of Dickens's language. Thomas Docherty seems to me partially correct in claiming that "Dickens does not want to make us see, but to make us learn how to see."[17] He is right to note Dickens's interest in the process and problems of visualization: interwoven with the attempt to "make us see" are reminders of the difficulties of seeing and warnings about the sorts of information that can and cannot reliably be drawn from the visual image. But beneath the confident surface, Dickens's descriptive style raises questions about the possibility of learning "how to see" in any final or utterly trustworthy sense. Perhaps the lesson, in the end, is that the most expert act of seeing is one that recognizes its own limitations.

Let me emphasize the essential point here: my argument is not that Dickens lacks skill or assurance as a descriptive artist, but that his language suggests serious doubts about the potential for any observer to extract reliable meaning from the external world and for any writer to represent the truth in words. Perhaps his great confidence in his skills actually exacerbated these doubts, since his own inability to interpret or represent satisfactorily would have revealed to him a more pervasive problem—if he could not succeed, with all his gifts, who could? In this sense my version of Dickens is the exact opposite of that presented several decades ago by J. Hillis Miller, who wrote that "[t]he special quality of Dickens' imagination is his assumption that he can get behind the surface by describing all of it bit by bit. . . . And when enough of the isolated parts are described, and their relations are discovered, the truth behind each, it may be, will be liberated."[18]

17. Docherty, *(Absent) Character,* 19.
18. Miller, *World,* xvi.

More characteristic of Dickens than this optimistic assumption is the whisper of uncertainty in Miller's own "it may be." Dickens's *desire* to liberate the truth through surface description is continually frustrated by his doubts about whether such a liberation is possible.

George Levine has argued that similar doubts typify the English realistic tradition,[19] though what may separate the greatest novelists—Dickens and George Eliot—from the rest is the depth of their uncertainty about what can be accomplished in their chosen form. Levine refers to Eliot's "collapse of faith in the dominant reality of the empirically verifiable," a collapse seen in *Middlemarch* when Will Ladislaw insists that "the true seeing is within" and that verbal and especially visual portraits of human beings can never capture the ambiguity and elusiveness of the represented object. In *Daniel Deronda* Eliot might be extrapolating from Dickens's descriptive style when she writes that "[a]ttempts at description are stupid: who can all at once describe a human being? even when he is presented to us we can only begin that knowledge of his appearance which must be completed by innumerable impressions under differing circumstances. We recognize the alphabet; we are not sure of the language." The work of both Dickens and Eliot, according to Philip Weinstein, "reveals an internal resistance to its own premises," though "one formulation of Dickens' more capacious achievement is that his work manages (as Eliot's does not) to assimilate . . . its own fissures."[20] Whereas Eliot's doubts affect primarily the arguments and moral judgments of her narrators, Dickens's filter through his themes and images down to the very words in which he attempts to describe the world.

Though Dickens was rarely as explicit as Eliot in his narrative philosophizing, there are good reasons to believe that his use of uncertain descriptive language was, at least by the later stages of his

19. See Levine, *The Realistic Imagination*, 8–12. Levine's view of Dickens in particular, articulated more fully in *Darwin*, is shifting and complicated. "Dickens," he writes, " . . . emphasizes the external rather than the internal, but only because he counts on the adequacy of the natural to express meaning. . . . [T]he emphasis on the external itself depends on strong confidence in the legibility of the material world, its expression of spiritual and moral realities comprehensible to those who choose to see." Yet this view, very similar to J. Hillis Miller's, is soon qualified: "nevertheless, Dickens's fiction does . . . [reveal] a growing uncertainty about the notion of an 'essential' self or about the possibility of detecting the moral through the physical." *Darwin*, 145–46.

20. George Levine, "Realism Reconsidered," 252; George Eliot, *Middlemarch*, 142; George Eliot, *Daniel Deronda*, 98; Weinstein, *Semantics*, 19.

career, a conscious act. One is simply its pervasiveness: eighteen of the
twenty extended physical descriptions of character in *Little Dorrit* are
obviously marked by the stylistic habits I have identified, some even
more strongly than the description of Maggy. The proportions are
comparable in the other long novels of Dickens's maturity. Uncertainty
is woven about equally throughout descriptions of men and women,
major and minor figures, the good and the evil, the honest and the
deceptive; the fact that Little Dorrit and Rigaud are described in the
same doubtful voice suggests that the problems of seeing are not
confined to cases in which individuals are trying deliberately to be
misleading. Sometimes the ambiguities and contradictions appear in
sufficient density to become the focus of a description, as in the long
introductory portrait of Miss Wade:

> She rose with the rest, and silently withdrew to a remote corner of the great
> room, where she sat herself on a couch in a window, seeming to watch the
> reflection of the water, as it made a silver quivering on the bars of the
> lattice. She sat, turned away from the whole length of the apartment, as
> if she were lonely of her own haughty choice. And yet it would have been
> as difficult as ever to say, positively, whether she avoided the rest, or was
> avoided.
>
> The shadow in which she sat, falling like a gloomy veil across her fore-
> head, accorded very well with the character of her beauty. One could hardly
> see the face, so still and scornful, set off by the arched dark eyebrows, and
> the folds of dark hair, without wondering what its expression would be
> if a change came over it. That it could soften or relent, appeared next to
> impossible. That it could deepen into anger or any extreme of defiance,
> and that it must change in that direction when it changed at all, would
> have been its peculiar impression upon most observers. It was dressed and
> trimmed into no ceremony of expression. Although not an open face, there
> was no pretence in it. (*LD*, 23–24)

Here everything works in concert to create a sense of visual and
interpretive uncertainty: the physical isolation, the shadowy room, the
tentative and hypothetical language, the open confessions of doubt.
Even the image of the reflected water, quivering and ephemeral, seems
to capture something of the observer's difficulty in seeing and understanding Miss Wade. It seems inconceivable that so thoroughly unclear
a moment could be anything but consciously arranged.

More telling, perhaps, are passages in which Dickens seems deliberately to be highlighting the potential for language to be unreliable and
insufficient. Tite Barnacle, who prefers "never, on any account whatever, to give a straightforward answer," replies to one of Clennam's

questions by acknowledging that "The Circumlocution Department, sir, . . . may have possibly recommended—possibly—I cannot say— that some public claim against the insolvent estate of a firm or copartnership to which this person may have belonged, should be enforced. The question may have been, in the course of official business, referred to the Circumlocution Department for its consideration. The Department may have either originated, or confirmed, a Minute making that recommendation" (*LD*, 112). The evasive words and phrases—may have, possibly, cannot say, or, should be—are precisely those that characterize Dickens's own descriptive prose, the unmistakable message here being that the connections between such language and any definite meaning are tenuous at best. Similarly, a proponent of "philosophical philanthropy" justifies the crimes of the villainous Rigaud by insisting that " 'It may have been his unfortunate destiny. He may have been the child of circumstances. It is always possible that he had, and has, good in him if one did but know how to find it out' " (*LD*, 127). Clennam, repressing his desire for Pet Meagles, asks himself after her excited response to Henry Gowan, "When has [he] seen her look like this? Not that there was any reason why he might, could, would, or should have even seen her look like this, or that he had ever hoped for himself to see her look like this: but still—when had he ever known her do it!" (*LD* 202). Ruth Bernard Yeazell has observed that the whole episode of "Nobody's Weakness," where nearly every word describes what is not the case, is couched in the "coy conditional."[21] And, as noted earlier, Mrs. Merdle underscores the significance of verb tense when she complains that her husband ought to be leaving his worries behind at work, "or seeming to. Seeming would be quite enough: I ask no more" (*LD*, 307). In each case Dickens appears almost to be parodying his own descriptive style in order to emphasize the potential for language to drift toward the relative, the possible. If such words are obviously untrustworthy when used by a Barnacle, philanthropist, or self-deceptive dreamer, how can they be relied upon when used by the narrator himself?

Dickens's doubts about the reliability of visual images are also conveyed in *Little Dorrit* through a long series of references, mostly negative, to painting and sculpture. Meisel writes that "[p]ictures, sculpture, and all that conduces to a fixed and frozen order do not

21. Yeazell, "Do It or Dorrit," 41.

enjoy an enviable repute in *Little Dorrit*" and cites at least a dozen disparaging allusions and pictorial metaphors. Casby and Tite Barnacle, Merdle and Lord Decimus, the Bosom and Mrs. General, are all characterized through references to paintings; Henry Gowan, "shallow and heartless,"[22] is a painter. One of Dickens's points seems to be that visual art, even more than linguistic art, relies wholly on appearance and therefore is liable to convey distorted or unreliable information. Near the end of the novel Pancks claims that " 'I am, in general, . . . a dry, uncomfortable, dreary Plodder and Grubber. That's your humble servant. There's his full-length portrait, painted by himself and presented to you, warranted a likeness!' " (*LD*, 801). Of course by this point the reader recognizes the "portrait" as nothing close to a "likeness" of Pancks. Earlier, in a passage more explicit about the representative inadequacies of painting, Clennam concludes "that many people select their models, much as the painters, just now mentioned, select theirs; and that, whereas in the Royal Academy some evil old ruffian of a Dog-stealer will annually be found embodying all the cardinal virtues, on account of his eyelashes, or his chin, or his legs (thereby planting thorns of confusion in the breasts of the more observant students of nature), so, in the great social Exhibition, accessories are often accepted in lieu of the internal character" (*LD*, 149). Here, in miniature, is Dickens's dilemma as a descriptive artist: how to move from accessories to internal character without getting snagged on the "thorns of confusion." It is not a dilemma he resolves to his own satisfaction.

The last word is left, appropriately, to the monstrous but articulate Rigaud, who gives voice to so much that the novel denies on the surface yet endorses in its images and themes. " 'Words, sir,' " he admonishes Clennam, " 'never influence the course of the cards, or the course of the dice. Do you know that? You do? I also play a game, and words are without power over it' " (*LD*, 745). Rarely has so subversive a statement about language been embedded in so massive a linguistic construction. Revealed consistently in Dickens's descriptive prose is his own fear that words, his medium and his passion, are without power to represent, interpret, and affect the world about which he writes.

The story of the evolution of Dickens's descriptive style is, with some qualification, one of increasing facility with language and diminishing

22. Meisel, *Realizations*, 315–17, 116.

faith in its efficacy. *Oliver Twist* may be unusually complicated for an early novel and *A Tale of Two Cities* unusually straightforward for a later one; and always Dickens's travel books and Christmas stories are less complex stylistically than his novels. But by and large the movement in the major fiction is from more direct and confident to more circuitous, hesitant, and polysemous descriptive language. One can nonetheless discover the beginnings of Dickens's eventual uncertainty even in his earliest writings. James Davies claims that the narrator of *Sketches by Boz* "struggles to make sense of his experiences and cannot hide the persisting uncertainty," calling him, "for all his street-wisdom and knowledge of London, . . . essentially an uncertain observer." In "Shabby-Genteel People," for instance, Davies finds tentative verbs such as "appears" and "seems," passages of the "sustained conditional," and everywhere language that "undermine[s] the Narrator's . . . confidently categorical assertions."[23] These are the earliest signs of a conflict between surface confidence and underlying uncertainty that will later become more pervasive.

A close look at the descriptive prose of *The Pickwick Papers* confirms on a linguistic level the general sense that it is unique among Dickens's novels in its unity of purpose. This is not to say that the text is without forces that contrast with and work to undermine its dominant mood: the interpolated tales, as Karen Chase points out, represent an "implicit challenge" to the central narrative, and the episodes in the Fleet qualify the optimism of the early and concluding adventures. But the self-divisive impulses in this first novel are carefully isolated, almost quarantined, away from the story's heart, and the overall tone remains hopeful and assured. The novel's language is not only exuberant and abundant but unhesitant, suffused most of the time with a confidence in its own ability to get things right. This is probably why Kincaid concludes that "in one novel, *The Pickwick Papers,* Dickens did often write in a manner to give some apparent support to the naive 'cinematic' idea. One can locate passages that not only appear to provide clear and uncomplicated details but also to give directions as to the angle from which we are to view these details."[24] Here, for once, Dickens seems to resemble the prodigy in Bagehot's description.

23. James A. Davies, *Textual Life,* 9–10.
24. Karen Chase, *Eros and Psyche,* 29; Kincaid, "Viewing and Blurring," 96.

In the vast, densely populated world of *Pickwick* only the portraits of Jingle, Job Trotter, and the Rev. Mr. Stiggins are comparable linguistically to those of Maggy and Miss Wade. Not surprisingly, the three preeminent hypocrites and deceivers in the novel are represented in the most doubt-infected language, a stylistic move wholly consistent with the discord of their intrusion into the idyllic terrain of Muggleton and Dingley Dell. Of Stiggins, Dickens writes that "[t]o do the red-nosed man justice, he would have been very far from wise if he had entertained any such intention; for to judge from his appearance, he must have been possessed of a most desirable circle of acquaintance, if he could have reasonably expected to be more comfortable anywhere else" (*PP*, 366). This rapid movement through "would," "if," "must," "if," and "could," blurring the distinction between the actual and the hypothetical, anticipates Dickens's mature style. Here, however, the narrator seems capable of identifying and ultimately seeing through the deceptions. "The most extraordinary thing" about Job Trotter "was that he was contorting his face into the most fearful and astonishing grimaces that ever were beheld. Nature's handiwork never was disguised with such extraordinary artificial carving as the man had overlaid his countenance with in one moment" (*PP*, 316–17). To recognize such artificiality *as* artificial—a recognition not often possible in the later novels—is largely to defeat it.

More characteristic of *Pickwick* is the initial, surprisingly nondescript sketch of Sam Weller:

> He was habited in a coarse-striped waistcoat, with black calico sleeves and blue glass buttons; drab breeches and leggings. A bright red handkerchief was wound in a very loose and unstudied style round his neck, and an old white hat was carelessly thrown on the side of his head. There were two rows of boots before him, one cleaned and the other dirty, and at every addition he made to the clean row, he paused from his work and contemplated its results with evident satisfaction. (*PP*, 118)

Almost none of Weller's complexity is introduced in this portrait, and nowhere is there a sign that the observer is struggling to picture, interpret, or reconcile opposing details. The mood throughout is indicative, the only conjunction (used seven times in three sentences) is "and," and the only qualifier that communicates even mild hesitation is "evident." Even so tempting a subject as the waistcoat or the hat provokes no figurative language. Not until Weller begins to speak does he become complicated and memorable. This is typical of a novel where action and especially speech do far more to establish character than does physical description, and where seeing and describing are not especially problematic acts. No character of Weller's distinctiveness in *any* subsequent Dickens novel is pictured so casually.

Though *Oliver Twist* is virtually contemporaneous with *The Pickwick Papers,* it reveals a dramatic shift in Dickens's descriptive language and, because of its peculiarly divided nature, points forward to the style of the later fiction.[25] The descriptions of more than a dozen characters in the novel are colored by the language of uncertainty, and, more significant, many of these characters are not clearly duplicitous in the manner of Stiggins or Job Trotter. Already polysemous complexity is becoming so ingrained in Dickens's style as to manifest itself in descriptions regardless of the motivations or moral nature of the character being viewed. The caution is less about the appearance of any particular individual, as in *Pickwick,* than about the wisdom of trusting appearance—and representations of appearance—at all. Mr. Brownlow is "respectable-looking," surely no emphatic recommendation in a novel that has already presented the gentleman in the white waistcoat; he stands on the street "as if he were in his elbow chair" and looks round "as if he contemplated running away himself; which it is very possible he might have attempted to do . . . had not a police officer . . . at that moment made his way through the crowd" (*OT,* 65, 67–68). Conditionals, futurities, oppositional conjunctions, and qualifying verbs can be found not only in introductory descriptions of Fagin and the Artful Dodger but also in those of the Maylies, Losborne, and Grimwig as well. The contrast between *Pickwick* and *Oliver Twist* in this regard is particularly important for the light it sheds on the determinants of Dickens's style. His second novel is less secure in its values and moral judgments than its predecessor or even its immediate successors, and at the same time is less straightforward in its methods of description: the connection between attitude and language, between the sureness with which Dickens apprehends an object and the manner in which he pictures it, is here especially evident.

Oliver Twist also initiates one of Dickens's more noteworthy and recurrent descriptive habits: that of picturing beautiful heroines in language hesitant and uncertain even by his own standards. The

25. For discussions of the divided nature of *Oliver Twist,* see John Romano, *Dickens and Reality,* 119; Juliet McMaster, "Diabolic Trinity in *Oliver Twist*"; Larson, *Broken Scripture,* 68; Lankford, " 'Parish Boy's Progress' "; and Brian Rosenberg, "Language of Doubt."

tentativeness and obscurity that mark the description of Little Dorrit are part of a much larger pattern that encompasses virtually all of Dickens's female protagonists and begins with Rose Maylie:

> The younger lady was in the lovely bloom and spring-time of womanhood; at that age, when if ever angels be for God's good purposes enthroned in mortal forms, they may be, without impiety, supposed to abide in such as hers.
>
> She was not past seventeen. Cast in so slight and exquisite a mould; so mild and gentle; so pure and beautiful; that earth seemed not her element, nor its rough creatures her fit companions. The very intelligence that shone in her deep blue eyes, and was stamped upon her noble head, seemed scarcely of her age, or of the world; and yet the changing expression of sweetness and good humour, the thousand lights that played about the face, and left no shadow there; above all, the smile, the cheerful, happy smile, were made for Home, and fireside peace and happiness. (*OT,* 212)

Alongside the sentimentalized details—admittedly hard to take—lie the qualifiers ("seemed"), conditionals ("if"), futurities ("might"), oppositions ("yet"), and repetitions ("so . . . so . . . so") that characterize the language of doubt. Rose, however, is no fraud, and though surely "the novel does not endorse [her] pale virtue so persuasively" as Dickens may have intended,[26] the portrait is no covert attack on her divine purity. It speaks, rather, of a novelist—stricken by the recent death of Mary Hogarth—for whom such purity is frustratingly elusive. Because ideal female beauty is somehow, for Dickens, not fully of this world, its physical form is almost always described in uncertain, severely qualified language. The beauty is not the sum of its parts, but a transcendence of its parts; it seems, like Rose Maylie (and Little Dorrit), both at home in and alien to its environment, possessed of a quality neither definable nor capturable in language.

Rose Maylie signals the first appearance of a descriptive myopia Dickens never manages to correct: most of his heroines are marked, like *Martin Chuzzlewit*'s Mary Graham, by "an indefinable something" (*MC,* 29) that resists understanding, or are, like *Nicholas Nickleby*'s Madeline Bray, "shaded by a cloud" of darkness (*NN,* 188) that obscures vision. They are introduced "crouching timidly in a corner" (*DS,* 3), "almost hidden in [a] dark corner" (*LD,* 40), in an "obscurity . . . difficult to penetrate" (*TTC,* 18) in "a little basement" (*OMF,* 34), "mostly in shadow" (*ED,* 8). Glimpses are usually

26. Romano, *Dickens and Reality,* 120.

oblique, frames circumscribed by closets and corners, light deflected or dimmed, so that what cannot be seen or understood becomes as fully acknowledged in each description as what can. The insistency and intrusiveness of this struggle suggest, I think, that Dickens's well-documented failure with heroines results not merely from an automatic acceptance of societal norms or from a technical inadequacy, but also, and more interestingly, from a profound uncertainty about the possibility of depicting an evanescent quality beyond depiction. Nowhere, in any case, is an interpretive difficulty in any of these novels more immediately transformed into visual imprecision, and nowhere is the relationship between the effort to represent and the style of representation defined more clearly. Dickens cannot discover the source or significance of Rose Maylie's "lovely bloom," so he cannot describe it with confidence.

Nicholas Nickleby, The Old Curiosity Shop, and *Barnaby Rudge* together exemplify Dickens's early descriptive style: none is as thoroughly uncertain as *Oliver Twist,* yet in each the language of doubt extends well beyond the isolated occurrences in *The Pickwick Papers.* The most important stylistic difference between these novels and the later ones is that here descriptive uncertainty is still mostly associated with characters whose appearance is explicitly identified in the narrative as misleading. The highest concentration of tentative and self-contradictory language can be found in descriptions of evil or deceptive characters such as Ralph Nickleby and Squeers, Quilp and Sally Brass, the elder Chester and Gashford. The observation that the tears of *Nicholas Nickleby*'s Mr. Pluck "stood, or seemed to stand, in his eyes" (*NN,* 347), can safely be assumed to illuminate his hypocritical nature. Kindly figures like Smike and Charles Cheeryble are pictured with hesitation as well because their inner natures are, respectively, less pitiful and less childish than their appearance might lead a "casual observer" (a favorite phrase of Dickens) to believe. Implicit in this selective use of doubtful language is the faith that some appearances, if not many, may be clearly seen and reliably interpreted.

There is little implicit or explicit evidence of such faith in *Martin Chuzzlewit,* the first novel fully to manifest Dickens's mature descriptive style. Opinions about the place of *Martin Chuzzlewit* in Dickens's artistic development have been unusually varied, probably because it was written during the most significant transitional period in his career. Some, like John Lucas, judge it to mark the end of an initial phase; others, like Steven Marcus, the beginning of a later one; for J. Hillis

Miller it is among Dickens's darkest works, dramatizing a world in which "there is no possibility of perceiving progressive change," while for James Kincaid it is "Dickens's funniest novel."[27] *Martin Chuzzlewit*'s crucial role in the evolution of Dickens's style is suggested by Marcus's observation that here "[f]or the first time Dickens's narrative style becomes consciously mannered" and "the language itself seems an organ of perception, shaping the experience almost as soon as it is received."[28] Questions of language and of perception are in this novel intimately joined, and, because usually these questions are provoked by acts of deception, the prose is suffused with doubt and contradiction. Duplicity and selfishness seem the most consistent governing principles in human relations stretching across two continents and a wide range of social and economic classes: Old Martin, ostensibly good, cruelly deceives his nephew; Jonas deceives the sisters Charity and Mercy; Tigg deceives the rich, Scadder the poor, Jefferson Brick the Americans and Mr. Nadgett the British. The novel overflows with nonexistent voices, swindles, physical and psychological assaults, pretensions, together portraying a society of people "wholly enclosed in themselves, wholly secret, wholly intent on reflexive ends."[29] Even the most upright characters—Tom Pinch, Mark Tapley, Mary Graham— seem implicated in deceptions and misinterpretations more destructive than is initially apparent.

Subject infects style in *Martin Chuzzlewit*, meaning that more characters are described in doubtful terms than in any previous novel and that the descriptions themselves are more profoundly uncertain. No characters in Dickens are more continually "seeming" and acting "as if" than Pecksniff and Jonas Chuzzlewit. Good characters like Tom Pinch, who "was perhaps about thirty but . . . might have been almost any age between sixteen and sixty," and Mark Tapley, "a young fellow, of some five- or six-and-twenty, perhaps" (*MC*, 18, 65), are pictured with nearly as much hesitation as are the evil ones. Most revealing of all is the long and intricately constructed portrait of Mr. Nadgett the spy:

> He was a short, dried-up, withered, old man, who seemed to have secreted his very blood, for nobody would have given him credit for the possession of six ounces of it in his whole body. How he lived was a secret, where

27. See Lucas, *Melancholy Man,* 113–14; Marcus, *Pickwick,* 213; and Kincaid, *Rhetoric of Laughter,* 132.
28. Marcus, *Pickwick,* 215–16.
29. Miller, *World,* 104.

he lived was a secret, and even what he was was a secret. In his musty old pocket-book he carried contradictory cards, in some of which he called himself a coal-merchant, in others a wine-merchant, in others a commission-agent, in others a collector, in others an accountant—as if he really didn't know the secret himself. He was always keeping appointments in the city, and the other man never seemed to come. He would sit on 'Change for hours, looking at everybody who walked in and out, and would do the like at Garraway's and in other business coffee-houses, in some of which he would be occasionally seen drying a very damp pocket-handkerchief before the fire and still looking over his shoulder for the man who never appeared. He was mildewed, threadbare, shabby, always had flue upon his legs and back, and kept his linen so secret by buttoning up and wrapping over that he might have none—perhaps he hadn't. He carried one stained beaver glove, which he dangled before him by the forefinger as he walked or sat, but even its fellow was a secret. Some people said he had been bankrupt, others that he had gone an infant into an ancient Chancery suit which was still depending, but it was all a secret. He carried bits of sealing-wax and a hieroglyphical old copper seal in his pocket and often secretly indited letters in corner boxes of the trysting-places before mentioned, but they never appeared to go to anybody, for he would put them into a secret place in his coat and deliver them to himself weeks afterwards, very much to his own surprise, quite yellow. He was that sort of man that if he had died worth a million of money or had died worth two-pence halfpenny, everybody would have said it was just as they expected. And yet he belonged to a class, a race peculiar to the city, who are secrets as profound to one another as they are to the rest of mankind. (*MC*, 447–48)

Surely Dickens's attractiveness to critics is partly attributable to his gift for concentrating within a discrete image, passage, or episode his characteristic ideas and methods. Periodically the most subtle and deeply buried impulses explode to the surface, shedding light on a text or even a group of texts. The portrait of Nadgett reads like a primer on Dickens's stylistic uncertainty and a demonstration of the difference between abundance and descriptive precision. The calm, almost exaggerated exactness of the opening clause—"short, dried-up, withered, old"—is quickly undercut in the same sentence by the hesitation of "seems" and the doubt of "nobody would have given." What follows is a torrent of tentative verbs, conditionals, futurities, contradictory conjunctions, qualifiers, and incompatible alternatives. Twice sentences appear to collapse, as if under the weight of their own language, into dashes followed by confessions of ignorance. Six points of view other than the narrator's are described, yet none is granted any particular authority. The contradictory cards in the musty old pocketbook embody contradictory signals sent by appearance and behavior. Yet for all his exaggerated secrecy, Nadgett is less an anomaly than an extreme example: the relations proclaimed here between language and interpretive uncertainty remain constant, if less openly defined, throughout Dickens's work.

With some exceptions, Dickens's fiction after *Martin Chuzzlewit* reveals a high and gradually increasing level of uncertainty in descriptions of character. The exceptions themselves are revealing: his Christmas stories and other occasional short fiction rely more heavily on abbreviated physical sketches and straightforward language than do his novels, suggesting that descriptive uncertainty is most prevalent when Dickens's imagination is most fully engaged. *A Christmas Carol* and *The Chimes*, both roughly contemporaneous with *Martin Chuzzlewit*, share little of the longer fiction's stylistic richness and indirection. Less drastic exceptions are *Hard Times* and *A Tale of Two Cities*, neither of which includes Dickens's best or most characteristic work. Otherwise the language of doubt is prevalent in all the novels beginning with *Dombey and Son*, becoming most widespread in *Little Dorrit, Our Mutual Friend,* and *The Mystery of Edwin Drood.*

An indication of how deeply ingrained uncertainty has become in Dickens's later descriptive style is its persistence through dramatic changes in narrative person and tone. Neither David Copperfield nor Pip is precisely equivalent to Dickens's typical third-person narrator, yet through every stage of development each shares most of that narrator's distinguishing descriptive mannerisms. *Bleak House,* with its two distinctly different narrative voices, is even more illuminating. The third-person narrator is more knowing, ironic, and public than Esther Summerson, with more direct access to the internal lives of others; presumably she is less quick to be suspicious and disillusioned. Yet for all their dissimilarities, both lapse into the same language—Dickens's habitual language—when describing human appearance.[30] Introductory descriptions (divided about equally between the two) lead each to step out of character, Esther becoming more worldly and ingenious and the third-person narrator more expansive and metaphoric. Each, that

---

30. A number of critics have pointed out the subtle likenesses between the voices of Esther and the third-person narrator. Robert Newsome writes that "Esther . . . often falls into the voice of the other narrator," in *Dickens on the Romantic Side of Familiar Things:* Bleak House *and the Novel Tradition,* 87; and Steven Connor notes that each narrative "somehow includes or is marked with 'traces' of the other," in *Charles Dickens,* 84. Neither remarks specifically, however, on similarities in their descriptive styles.

is, moves closer to the other and to Dickens's characteristic descriptive voice. In consecutive chapters the third-person narrator introduces Lady Dedlock by noting that "[s]he is perfectly well-bred. If she could be translated to Heaven to-morrow, she might be expected to ascend without any rapture"; and Esther introduces her godmother by noting that "she was handsome; and if she had ever smiled, would have been (I used to think) like an angel—but she never smiled" (*BH*, 10, 15). Esther's descriptions of characters such as Mr. Krook, with his "breath issuing in visible smoke from his mouth, as if he were on fire within," and Mr. Turveydrop, with "such a neckcloth on . . . , that it seemed as though he must inevitably double up, if it were cast loose" (*BH*, 50, 190), would fit seamlessly into any of Dickens's third-person narratives.

What separates *Little Dorrit, Our Mutual Friend,* and *The Mystery of Edwin Drood* from Dickens's other novels is, more than anything else, the overt self-consciousness of his struggle with the difficulties of appearance and language. *Little Dorrit*'s moments of reflexivity are repeated, even expanded, in *Our Mutual Friend,* which virtually begins with a scene before the Veneerings's mirror that serves, as John Romano points out, as an "ambivalent and doubtful" emblem of the novelist's art. "Surface," Romano notes, "or rather a world that seems indeed to be all surface, is both satirized and unsmilingly disdained,"[31] as are forms of representation that attempt to re-create and draw meaning from surface images. The unsuccessful struggle to see and understand becomes, in this novel, openly the subject of many descriptions. The eyes of Mr. Venus "are like the over-tried eyes of an engraver, but he is not that; his expression and stoop are like those of a shoemaker, but he is not that" (*OMF,* 78). A parlour door opens to disclose Jenny Wren, "a child—a dwarf—a girl—a something—sitting on a little low old-fashioned arm-chair, which had a kind of little working bench before it" (*OMF,* 222). No longer content to confine uncertainty to the subtleties of style, Dickens has begun by this point to carry it regularly to the surface of the narrative, so that the frustrated observer of Mr. Venus or Jenny Wren bears almost no resemblance to the relaxed, assured observer of Sam Weller. The novel's many disguises and doublings are signs of the same distrust in the reliability, even stability, of appearance.

31. Romano, *Dickens and Reality,* 30–31.

Had *The Mystery of Edwin Drood* been completed, it almost certainly would have proven to be Dickens's most self-divided and linguistically complicated novel (not to mention the focal point of this book). Even as a fragment, with many of its relationships and themes unresolved, it suggests pretty clearly the direction in which Dickens was moving as a describer of character. More elliptical in style than both *Little Dorrit* and *Our Mutual Friend,* its descriptions are nonetheless packed with doubtful and hesitant language. Mr. Grewgious in particular is less a human figure than a cloud of possibility, with passages like the following accompanying each of his appearances: "His voice was as hard and dry as himself, and Fancy might have ground it straight, like himself, into high-dried snuff. And yet, through the very limited means of expression that he possessed, he seemed to express kindness. If Nature had but finished him off, kindness might have been recognizable in his face at this moment. But if the notches in his forehead wouldn't fuse together, and if his face would work and couldn't play, what could he do, poor man!" (*ED,* 87). Phrases like "a certain air" and "an indefinable kind" recur obsessively: the Landlesses alone have "something untamed about them," "a certain air . . . of hunter and huntress," "a certain air of being the objects of the chase," and "an indefinable kind of pause . . . in their whole expression" (*ED,* 56–57); Grewgious has "something dreamy" about him, Bazzard "a general air of having been reared under [a] shadow," Dick Datchery "something of a military air," Mrs. Billickin "the air of having been expressly brought-to" for languishing (*ED,* 123, 114, 206, 249). Again there is a high degree of self-consciousness about both the unreliability of appearance and, especially, the slippery nature of language, with the narrator more than once drawing attention to the ambiguity or inadequacy of his own expressions. Grewgious seems "apparently— if such a word can be used of one who had no apparent lights or shadows about him—complimented by [a] question" (*ED,* 92); and, in the last chapter Dickens ever wrote, Princess Puffer "seems . . . to begin making herself ready for sleep. . . . But seeming may be false or true" (*ED,* 270). At such moments the language itself appears more interesting to Dickens than character, setting, or plot.

The evolution of Dickens's descriptive style, finally, reveals no abrupt sea change but a gradual strengthening of tendencies present from the start. The early novels contain, but evade or deny, challenges to their own stance of assurance and authority; the later novels more often acknowledge and reflect openly on those challenges. Initially

Dickens rests his faith, as he probably must, on his own ability to decipher appearance and to create its linguistic equivalent; eventually neither his eyes nor his voice seems up to the task, suggesting some loss of self-confidence but, more important, a heightened sensitivity to the challenges of vision and representation. In *The Pickwick Papers* the guests of the Wardles are pictured easily and unhesitantly because there is no sense of separation among the acts of seeing, understanding, and describing. Mr. Pickwick, standing in for his creator, has "leisure to observe the appearance, and speculate upon the characters and pursuits, of the persons by whom he [is] surrounded" (*PP,* 67). In *Our Mutual Friend* the "great looking-glass above the sideboard" (*OMF,* 10) intervenes between the reader and the guests of the Veneerings, "reflecting" in a more mechanical sense than Pickwick and embodying, in its flatness and circumscribing frame, all that vision and representation cannot do.

"Characters in fiction," writes William Gass, "are mostly empty canvas. I have known many who have passed through their stories without noses, or heads to hold them; others have lacked bodies altogether, exercised no natural functions, possessed some thoughts, a few emotions, but no psychology, and apparently made love without the necessary organs."[32] This playful but accurate observation suggests that the notion of a cinematic or all-seeing Dickens overlooks, among other things, the high degree of selectivity in all literary representation and draws attention away from the tendencies and principles directing the process of selection. It may be true, as Baruch Hochman argues, that "literature, despite the relative meagerness of the information it provides, has the potential for projecting coherent and meaningful images of people,"[33] yet it remains nonetheless important to attend to the given details out of which those fuller images are constructed. For all their particularity, Dickens's characters are, to be sure, mostly empty canvas, and the portions that are painted in often generate yet another tension in the nature of those characters—this time between what might be called familiarity and strangeness, or typicality and idiosyncracy.

In one sense there is nothing new about this argument. More than thirty years ago John Bayley wrote that "[t]he natural characters, the

32. Gass, *Fiction,* 45.
33. Hochman, *Character,* 62.

Iagos, Beckys, and Micawbers, are both universally recognizable as types and yet completely unique as individuals. It is on this paradox that the characters of Nature . . . are solidly founded." Even earlier David Cecil had insisted that "Mr. Pecksniff is not only Mr. Pecksniff, he is the type of all hypocrites; Mrs. Jellyby is not only Mrs. Jellyby, . . . she is also the type of all professional philanthropists."[34] My concern, however, is less with the resemblance of Dickens's characters to actual types (ultimately an unresolvable issue) than with Dickens's overt invitations for the reader to consider his characters as both typical and unusual—or, better, to offer and then withdraw or qualify the prospect of typicality. The physical details Dickens presents and the rhetoric with which he surrounds them intensify the sense of uncertainty created by other elements of his descriptive language by swinging characters between the poles of similarity and difference.

One can observe this throughout *Little Dorrit:* Maggy's face bears an expression "which is seen in the faces of the blind"; Rigaud has "much of the expression of a wild beast"; Old Nandy seems a man "anybody may pass, any day, on the thronged thoroughfares of the metropolis" (*LD*, 100, 3, 363). But Maggy is not blind, Rigaud's eyes are too closely set to be beastlike, Nandy is a collection of idiosyncrasies. More fully developed is the combined typicality/individuality of the Italian vagrant Cavalletto, who is pictured several times in the opening chapter of the novel:

> A sunburnt, quick, lithe, little man, though rather thick-set. Earrings in his brown ears, white teeth lighting up his grotesque brown face, intensely black hair clustering about his brown throat, a ragged red shirt open at his brown breast. Loose, seaman-like trousers, decent shoes, a long red cap, and a red sash round his waist, and a knife in it.

> The little man sat down again upon the pavement with the negligent ease of one who was thoroughly accustomed to pavements; and placing three hunks of coarse bread before himself . . . began contentedly to work his way through them as if to clear them off were a sort of game.

> John Baptist answered with that peculiar back-handed shake of the right forefinger which is the most expressive negative in the Italian language. . . .
>   "Altro!" returned John Baptist, closing his eyes and giving his head a vehement toss.

> . . . in his ready sleep, in his fits and starts, altogether a true son of the land that gave him birth. (*LD*, 4, 7, 8, 14)

---

34. Bayley, *Characters of Love*, 280; Cecil, *Early Victorian Novelists*, 58.

As a result of repetition, extended examination, or novelty, eight significant details seem to stand out in these relatively brief descriptions
of Cavalletto: his swarthy complexion, his red clothing, his smallness,
his quick, fitful movements, his finger gesture, his all-purpose use of
"altro," his way of sitting, and his way of eating bread. These are
repeated, together or in part, nearly every time he reappears in the
novel. With about half of these details Dickens invites the reader to
align Cavalletto with a group: his movements show him to be a "true
son of the land that gave him birth," his finger gesture is an unspoken
part of the Italian language, and his size and complexion are typically
Mediterranean. Other details, especially the habitual use of "altro,"
establish him as eccentric or idiosyncratic. The difference here between
Dickens and other novelists is, again, less in kind than in degree. While
others balance characters between the typical and the individual, Dickens defines the relevance of both categories with unusual explicitness
and provides evidence of both that is unusually extreme.

The history of response to Dickens's characters reveals that his
juxtaposed claims of typicality and individuality have managed to
provoke competing reactions, ranging from Henry James's complaint
that Dickens's people are "particular without being general, . . . individuals without being types," to the more recent assessment that
"[a]t moments any Dickens reader will recognize that he has left
the realms of realism behind and entered a *Pilgrim's Progress*-like
world of giant symbols."[35] Perpetually, it seems, the critical pendulum
has swung between the views that Dickens's characters are "nearly
all individuals and not types" and that they "symboliz[e] . . . eternal
verities," with the occasional mediating claim that they "have each
the roundness of individual reality combined with generalization."[36]
More than merely differences of opinion, these opposed judgments
are alternative responses to deliberately contradictory signals. Here as
elsewhere in Dickens, judiciously selective readers can find powerful
support for utterly incompatible interpretations. Unlike critics such
as Bayley, I do not see the elements of typicality and individuality
as blending together into a natural whole, but rather as coexisting
uncomfortably, or even clashing. The reader is drawn not toward a
moderate center, but simultaneously toward opposite extremes.

35. James, *Theory of Fiction*, 202; Jane Vogel, *Allegory in Dickens*, 42.
36. George H. Ford, *Dickens and His Readers: Aspects of Novel-Criticism since
1836*, 137; Arthur Machen, "The Art of Dickens," 666; Horne, *New Spirit*, 21.

Like Dickens's detailed yet uncertain descriptive language, his blending of the typical and individual creates an expectation for the recognizable and accessible that is never fulfilled. Figures who appear tangibly present and reassuringly similar to clearly defined types are at the same time elusive, blurred, and unique. Maggy can and cannot be seen, can and cannot be categorized. Surely this is among the important reasons for the endless critical debates about the realism of Dickens's characters, for their immediately recognizable distinctiveness, and for the assessment, not so easily dismissed, that "generations of readers have reacted to [them] as if they were living persons"[37]—a statement whose ambiguity is worthy of Dickens himself and whose crucial word, clearly, is "reacted." Open and familiar on the one hand, hidden and mysterious on the other, his characters re-create the paradox of connection and separation that haunts all human relations.

37. Doris Alexander, *Creating Characters with Charles Dickens*, 3.

4

SECOND NATURE
The Fragmentation of Personality

A sullen, passionate girl! Her rich black hair was all about her, her face was flushed and hot, and as she sobbed and raged, she plucked at her lips with an unsparing hand.

"Selfish brutes!" said the girl, sobbing and heaving between whiles. "Not caring what becomes of me! Leaving me here hungry and thirsty and tired, to starve, for anything they care! Beasts! Devils! Wretches!" (*LD,* 25–26)

THE MOST EXTENSIVE set-piece in the second chapter of *Little Dorrit* is devoted not to Clennam or Mr. Meagles or even Miss Wade but, somewhat surprisingly, to Tattycoram, a figure about whom critics have had relatively little to say beyond a passing reference or mild complaint.[1] To be sure, Tattycoram is one of those characters in Dickens who lingers around the fringes of the narrative and fails to measure up to realistic standards of interiority, development, and proportionality—presumably an instance of what Henry James dismisses as "nothing but figure." Her internal life, such as it is, appears to be painted in broad strokes and is explained, by Tattycoram herself, in direct and explicit terms. The passionate temperament introduced at the start never evolves in any meaningful way, though it is superficially cooled following her repentant, even self-abasing return to the Meagleses' cottage—an abrupt move that provides little satisfaction to the reader or, one would suppose, Tattycoram. Surely her sobbing and heaving and melodramatic hurling of epithets exemplify what William Dean Howells means by "disproportioned" and "overcharged," or what Lionel Trilling has in mind when noting the absence of "autonomous life" in the secondary characters of *Little*

---

1. J. C. Reid's complaint about the absence of "literary tact" in the highly moralistic presentation of Tattycoram is typical. See *Charles Dickens: Little Dorrit,* 40.

Dorrit.[2] Even allowing for her subsidiary role in the novel, Tattycoram must be considered a failure when judged as a representation of a complete, believably imagined human personality.

But of course that is not the way she must be judged, nor are realistic criteria the only ones appropriate for gauging the subtlety and effectiveness of a fictional character. Tattycoram is a clear, if not necessarily spectacular, example of Dickens's typical manner of representing emotion and psychology. In place of carefully delineated shades of character there is stark self-division; in place of a discrete, rounded consciousness there is a fragment of a larger whole encompassing several different individuals. Not in herself a complex personality, Tattycoram is part of the larger presentation of personality in *Little Dorrit* that is in the end elaborate and complex. She is a reminder that, when discussing the representation of human nature in Dickens, one must always distinguish between the portraits of particular figures and the more extensive picture that emerges when those figures are considered as an interconnected group. What I am suggesting goes well beyond the traditional notion of the Jamesian "ficelle," or limited character who exists to shed light on larger, more central personalities;[3] rather than illuminating a personality outside herself, Tattycoram forms a crucial part of a personality (or personalities) encompassing a cluster of characters. She reveals too that Dickens's treatment of what he calls in *Little Dorrit* "the internal character" (*LD,* 149) is as fraught with oppositions and unresolved tensions as is his treatment of physical appearance.

Tattycoram is from the start riven down the middle, with her first action, appropriately, not a whole but a "half curtsey" (*LD,* 17). Her name, to whose history Dickens devotes nearly a page, is both one-half of an opposed pair and itself a combination of ill-fitting alternatives: the Meagleses have substituted "Tattycoram" for "Harriet Beadle," her institutional name (and a prior, "arbitrary" [*LD,* 18] substitution for her unknown family name); "Tattycoram" weds the alternatives "Tatty"—a playful substitution for "Hatty," itself a substitution for "Harriet"—and "Coram," the name of the originator of the foundling home. "At one time she was Tatty," Mr. Meagles explains, "and at one time she was Coram, until we got into a way of mixing the two names

2. James, *Theory of Fiction,* 213; Howells, *Criticism and Fiction,* 82; Trilling, Introduction, xv.

3. See, for instance, James, *Theory of Fiction,* 219–26.

together, and now she is always Tattycoram" (*LD*, 19)—that is, an awkward mixture.

The division in Tattycoram's name extends to her social and familial roles and, most dramatically, to her internal life, where "the fury of the contest in the girl" produces a "bodily struggle . . . as if she were rent by the Demons of old" (*LD*, 26). Ambiguously poised between adopted child and servant, sister and maid, she is treated by all three Meagleses with a mixture of solicitude and condescension. Rather than gliding along some gradually altering scale, her responses swing between the extremes of gratitude and self-effacement on the one hand and bitter resentment and self-assertion on the other. Within moments she can call the Meagleses "selfish brutes" and then acknowledge that "[t]hey are nothing but good to me. I love them dearly" (*LD*, 26–27)—and wholeheartedly mean all she says. Her shifts between states are less like normal alterations in mood than like the monstrous transformations of the werewolf or Jekyll/Hyde: Pet Meagles, like the frightened heroine in a tale of horror, tells the angry version of Tattycoram to "take your hands away. I feel as if some one else was touching me!" (*LD*, 196). Mr. Meagles's repeated admonition that Tattycoram "count five-and-twenty" (*LD*, 117) resembles a warning about some talismanic chant whose omission results in a terrible change. And Tattycoram's own plea to Miss Wade—"Go away from me, go away from me! When my temper comes upon me, I am mad" (*LD*, 27)—recalls the tortured, self-conscious cries of the human being about to metamorphosize into the beast.

Appearances notwithstanding, Tattycoram's is no tale of extreme halves being subsumed in the end into a stable, integrated whole, but instead a confirmation of Robert Higbie's claim that Dickens values the "very inability [of his characters] to resolve their tension, to exercise rational control." Her sudden, apologetic return to the Meagleses as a changed woman actually reveals no change at all, only, perhaps, a more concerted effort to battle her darker side that generates what John Kucich terms an "illusory synthesis."[4] Her final emotional outpouring is not cleansing or celebratory but "half in exultation and half in despair, half in laughter and half in tears" (*LD*, 810), signaling the persistence of the old self-division. Given Dickens's sensitivity to the difference between certainty and possibility, her final remarks are

---

4. Higbie, *Character and Structure*, 163; Kucich, *Repression*, 208.

anything but definitive: "I only mean to say, that, after what I have gone through, I hope I shall never be quite so bad again, and that I shall get better by very slow degrees. I'll try very hard" (*LD,* 811).

Nearly as indivisible as Tattycoram's two halves are those ties to other characters that place her fragmentary internal life into a larger, more meaningful context. Michael Squires has noted that she is paired with Pet Meagles in a relationship that clarifies the nature and limitations of both characters.[5] The extremities of behavior in Tattycoram explain, and are explained by, the more moderate and repressed behavior of Pet. The maid's hysterical bouts of self-denial and self-assertion frame, as it were, the mistress's gentler mixture of modesty and self-indulgence, a mixture that might be missed were it not for the clarifying presence of Tattycoram: where one hurls epithets, the other marries Henry Gowan in spite of her parents' disapproval; and where one tears her own flesh, the other worries that her betrothal "seems so neglectful . . . , so unthankful" (*LD,* 335). Together the two enact, in a major and minor key, comparably ambivalent emotional responses to the smothering care of Mr. and Mrs. Meagles. In place, that is, of a single character whose personality is fluid and complex, Dickens presents a pair of simpler, relatively static, mutually illuminating characters who together form a more complex unit.

Eventually Tattycoram is drawn from her pairing with Pet Meagles into a second pairing with her more obvious double, Miss Wade, to whom she refers—in one of Dickens's more psychologically and sexually evocative phrases—as "my own self grown ripe" (*LD,* 811). If the first relationship reveals Tattycoram's split personality to be an extreme version of a more moderate and believable ambivalence, the second reveals it to be an early or immature version of a debilitating neurosis. Tattycoram is as important to an understanding of Miss Wade's origins as is the interpolated "History of a Self-Tormentor," and Miss Wade in turn dramatizes the possible consequences of Tattycoram's self-division. In the older woman the struggle between the desire for love and the rejection of pity has formed a personality dominated by self-loathing and implacable resentment. Again Dickens does with a pair of characters what some novelists might do with one: rather than allowing Tattycoram herself to evolve, he embodies one

5. See Squires, "Dickens's Imagination," 51.

potential version of her evolution in a second figure who is virtually a second self.

Extend Tattycoram's example throughout *Little Dorrit,* throughout many other novels very like *Little Dorrit* in this regard, and one senses how personality is typically presented in Dickens's fiction. Two traits especially characterize his depiction of internal life: the tendency to present characters who are self-divided or fragmented in a variety of ways, and the tendency to form what Squires calls "complex configuration[s] of human relationships" in which relatively incomplete or fragmentary characters bind together into a multifaceted whole. Both tendencies have been remarked upon recently by critics including Squires, Kucich, Higbie, and Karen Chase, but the combined effects of the two have in my view been insufficiently noted.[6] By creating characters that are both divided into incompatible sections and dependent portions of larger psychological structures, Dickens conveys the impression that personality is rarely whole, coherent, or autonomous, and certainly that no individual can grasp the personality of another in anything but a fragmentary way. This is an impression consistent with modern psychoanalysis, which "in its more radical implications," Chase observes, "overthrows the sovereignty of the integral subject, allowing us to conceive the personality not as an atomistic unit but as a play of complex and competing processes, structures of relative autonomy which function as psychological agents but not as psychological wholes." It is also, as Jay Clayton has pointed out, a provocative anticipation of the postmodern "deconstruction of the subject" seen in novelists such as Pynchon and Barth.[7] Far more than do the rounded characters traditionally celebrated by mimetic criticism, Dickens's fragments undermine the belief in personality as an atomistic unit and foreground the competition among related but distinctly independent processes. Rarely do his characters create the illusion of psychological completeness and rarely do they surprise, in E. M. Forster's sense, by revealing unexpected yet appropriate aspects of personality. What surprise there is comes from the utter incompatibility of impulses contained within a single consciousness,

6. See Squires, "Dickens's Imagination," 50–52; Kucich, *Repression,* 219–52; Higbie, *Character and Structure,* 126; and Chase, *Eros and Psyche,* 32–38. The previous quotation is from Squires, "Dickens's Imagination," 51.

7. Chase, *Eros and Psyche,* 32; Jay Clayton, "Dickens and the Genealogy of Postmodernism," 187–88.

or from the doggedness with which a character enacts and reenacts the same psychological or emotional pattern.

The assumption underlying assessments of character in realistic fiction has generally been that an author's understanding of human nature is revealed through—and the reader's respect for that understanding is dependent upon—the creation of imaginary individuals each of whom imitates an "actual" individual. The more complex and rounded the fictional personality, the more astute the novelist's grasp of real personality, and the richer and more appreciative the response of the reader. Such an assumption implies, first, that human personality is to a considerable degree definable and therefore reproducible, whereas, as Fred Kaplan observes, the operative assumption in Dickens's fictional world is "that our most extraordinary qualities are ultimately inexplicable."[8] It also ignores some of the most important and obvious differences between the textual and extratextual realms: the former, because it is more highly structured, limited, and overtly controlled than the latter, invites a different understanding of personality. Connections among individuals are more easily and firmly drawn, the boundaries of individual consciousness more easily crossed, comparable or contrasting forms of behavior more easily juxtaposed. Complexity becomes a collective rather than an individual characteristic. Dickens's manner of representing personality is highly "novelistic" in the sense that it acknowledges and takes advantage of the peculiarities and potentialities of the form: his fragmentation of consciousness within characters, Kucich notes, leads "personality [to be] expanded as seemingly incompatible impulses are brought into conjunction," and his dispersal of traits among clusters of characters allows him to explore what Chase calls "a range of response not available to individuals."[9] Both comments suggest that Dickens's freedom from (or indifference to) the need to represent complete individual personalities enables him to anatomize more fully the nature of personality itself and to construct characters that can be considered (as realistic novels themselves can be considered) not equivalents but illuminating alternatives to reality.

The starkness of Tattycoram's self-division and the clarity of its portrayal near the start of *Little Dorrit* make her a paradigm against

---

8. Fred Kaplan, *Dickens and Mesmerism: The Hidden Springs of Fiction,* 236.
9. Kucich, *Repression,* 240; Chase, *Eros and Psyche,* 38.

which many other fragmented characters can be measured. Certainly both her general struggle between opposing impulses and her more specific fluctuation between self-denial and self-assertion recur frequently throughout the novel. Miss Wade's " 'self-tormenting' oscillation between masochistic self-destruction and hunger for power" is, as I have already suggested, a more malignant version of Tattycoram's own schism.[10] Pancks's separation of his businesslike and humane selves—a form of splitting especially recurrent in Dickens[11]—is so extreme as to generate a masochism of its own, each side belittling and dismissing the other until, after the financial ruin of Clennam, he explodes into verbal and physical self-abuse:

> . . . Mr. Pancks took hold of himself by the hair of his head, and tore it in desperation at the spectacle.
> "Reproach me!" cried Pancks. "Reproach me, sir, or I'll do myself an injury. Say, You fool, you villain. Say, Ass, how could you do it, Beast, what did you mean by it! Catch hold of me somewhere. Say something abusive to me!" All the time, Mr. Pancks was tearing at his tough hair in a most pitiless and cruel manner. (*LD*, 712)

One version of Pancks apprehends and punishes the other, an act that accords perfectly with Tattycoram's "pluck[ing] at her lips with an unsparing hand," or Miss Wade's "self-torment," or Mrs. Clennam's maniacal asceticism, or any of the other instances of self-inflicted pain in the novel. The prevalence and variety of masochism in *Little Dorrit* arise less from characters that loathe themselves than from characters made up of multiple selves that loathe and look to subvert one another.

Tattycoram and Pancks especially represent divided personalities in which one side—her grateful one, his humane one—seems, in the moral scheme of the novel, obviously the more attractive and sympathetic. The ambiguous example of Jeremiah Flintwinch, however, may be more typical: "His neck was so twisted, that the knotted ends of his white cravat usually dangled under one ear; his natural acerbity and energy, always contending with a second nature of habitual repression, gave his features a swollen and suffused look; and altogether, he had a weird appearance of having hanged himself at one time or other, and of having gone about ever since, halter and all, exactly as some timely hand had cut him down" (*LD*, 37). The pattern of fragmentation

---

10. Kucich, *Repression*, 236.
11. See Barbara Lecker, "The Split Characters of Charles Dickens."

defined through Tattycoram and Pancks is here followed precisely: both the energy and the repression, the self-assertion and self-denial, are "natural," or parts of Flintwinch's essential being. The relationship between these two natural selves is perpetually contentious, ending neither in the triumph of one nor in the combination of the two into a more uniform whole. Again the division leads, at least emblematically, to an act of self-mutilation: note that Flintwinch has the appearance of "having hanged himself," not of having been hanged by someone else. In this instance, though, the reader is encouraged to endorse neither the energetic nor the repressed self, the one being aggressive and dangerous and the other passive yet, in its malicious secrecy, equally dangerous. Less Jekyll/Hyde than Hyde/Hyde, Flintwinch—like his partner and counterpart Mrs. Clennam—may be partially neutralized as a destructive force by his ongoing internal warfare.

In a novel so "preoccupied" as *Little Dorrit* with the structure and limitations of storytelling,[12] it is not surprising to find many fragmented characters constructing narratives in which some partial or alternative self plays a central role. Thus two sides of the same personality are connected yet distinctly separated as narrator/character, observer/participant, reality/fiction. Clennam's ongoing saga of "Nobody"—"Why should he be vexed or sore at heart? It was not his weakness that he had imagined. It was nobody's, nobody's within his knowledge, why should it trouble him?"—is a clear example of such self-divisive storytelling, as is Little Dorrit's tale of the Princess and the "poor little tiny woman" (*LD*, 200, 293). As if to underscore the connection between these two stories of repression, and to make it clear that the desiring figure in Clennam's narrative is precisely the one desired in Little Dorrit's, Dickens echoes the language of the former in the latter, where "nobody missed" the shadow guarded by the little woman, "nobody was the worse for it"; eventually there is "nobody to look at" the Princess and "nobody for her to look at" (*LD*, 294).[13] Typically, in an internalized version of the self-abuse of Tattycoram and Pancks, both fictions conclude with the destruction of one side

12. Metz, "Blighted Tree," 222. Janice M. Carlisle too has discussed the centrality of the fictional form in *Little Dorrit*, calling the novel "a thorough exploration of the concept of fiction from its original root meaning to its modern use as a label for a literary form." See "*Little Dorrit*: Necessary Fictions," 211.

13. According to John Forster, of course, Dickens's original title for *Little Dorrit* was *Nobody's Fault*. See *The Life of Charles Dickens*, vol. 2, 179.

of the personality by the other, Clennam symbolically drowning the disappointed Nobody and Little Dorrit killing off the forlorn little woman. As Janice Carlisle has observed, Little Dorrit becomes at the conclusion of her narrative "a corpse united to a shadow."[14]

Less rigorously controlled fictions are constructed by William Dorrit and Flora Finching. Dorrit's "Father of the Marshalsea" is an alternative self with an imaginary past and imaginary importance through which he maintains the self-esteem crushed by decades in the debtor's prison. Periodically, as when he receives gifts from departing collegians, he refers to the Father in the third person—" 'My good sir, . . . he is infinitely obliged to you' " (*LD, 66*)—consigning humiliation to an alter ego as Clennam and Little Dorrit consign desire and disappointment. Flora's second self, a recollected version of her own younger self, has no official title, but serves too as a shield against frustration and a channel for repressed desire. Her entry into the novel as "a caricature of her girlish manner, such as a mummer might have presented at her own funeral" (*LD, 130*), for all its loud comedy, has a distinctly Flintwinchian air of morbidity, continuing the by-now-familiar pattern of one self tormenting or murdering the other. That the Father of the Marshalsea and Flora Finching are more unstable than Clennam and Little Dorrit (though no more fragmented) is indicated by their inability to keep the boundaries between alternative selves, or the relationship between narrator and character, clearly defined. "How are we to know," James Kincaid asks, "the dancer from the dance, the past Flora Finching from the present article, from the performance she gives, the roles she plays?"[15] Indeed, how are we to know that one side of Flora is in fact a performance or role and not, like the repressed Flintwinch, a second, natural version of her essential self?

One can distinguish between the complex role-playing of these fragmented characters and the simpler version enacted by villains such as Casby and Rigaud, whose personalities are undivided and comparatively unambiguous. Casby's role as the Patriarch is little more than an efficacious facade, "a mere Inn sign-post without any Inn" (*LD, 149*); no portion of his actual nature is embodied by or expressed through his beaming exterior. There is never any possibility of Casby or the reader confusing one role with the other, or of the two being fused into a single temperament, but instead an inexorable movement toward

14. Carlisle, "Necessary Fictions," 202.
15. Kincaid, "Performance," 12–13.

his unmasking (or shearing) by Pancks. No portion of Tattycoram, Flintwinch, or Flora could be excised to reveal the "truth" because the truth includes the competing and contradictory traits. Similarly, Rigaud's incarnations as Lagnier and Blandois act as disguises rather than as alternate selves and suggest no split in his character. He remains always in control of his various identities and aware of their essential singularity, referring to himself openly, in the end, as "Rigaud Lagnier Blandois" (*LD*, 786). The truly fragmented character in Dickens, the one subject to what Elaine Showalter terms "the chaos of identity,"[16] is unable or unwilling to make this synthesis: even after acknowledging their love, Clennam and Little Dorrit remain unprepared to imagine themselves as Clennam/Nobody and Little Dorrit/Poor Little Woman; even after climactic moments of self-description, Tattycoram and Flora continue to be polarized into contentious selves.

The internal organization of so many characters in *Little Dorrit*, whereby competing fragments are held together in uneasy alliance, is, as I have suggested, analogous to the organization among groups of characters, whereby figures who are themselves fragments cohere into units that form complex "group" personalities. The effect, again, is to emphasize the tension and disarray concealed beneath the seeming coherence of identity and to explore varieties of response implausible within a single individual. The novel is filled with pairs of dissimilar and even antagonistic characters who are, paradoxically, bound together into a larger unit, including Rigaud and Cavalletto, Casby and Pancks, Flora and Mr. F's Aunt, and Little Dorrit and Maggy. Showalter has defined similar roles for Mr. F's Aunt and Maggy, the one serving as "the embodiment of Flora's repressed anger at Arthur's rejection" and the other as an incarnation of "Little Dorrit's physical, aggressive, and uninhibited self."[17] More generally, both Mr. F's Aunt and Maggy clarify and contextualize the behavior of their alter egos, just as Tattycoram does for Pet Meagles and Miss Wade. Like Rigaud's "monstrous shadow imitating him on the wall and ceiling" (*LD*, 445), the more marginal character gives exaggerated, frightening, but revealing shape to the internalized, obliquely suggested responses of the more central.

Pancks and Cavalletto form parallel pairings with Casby and Rigaud respectively. In each case a subservient figure is bound to a

16. Showalter, "Guilt," 26.
17. Ibid., 37, 35.

domineering one, a divided personality is manipulated by a unified one, a servant loathes yet remains magnetically drawn to a complacent master. Both relationships are eerily symbiotic: Casby and Rigaud need unquestioning obedience, while Pancks and Cavalletto need equally strongly, if less consciously, to *be* obedient. Only because each finds an alternative master—Clennam for Cavalletto, Clennam and Little Dorrit both for Pancks—can the original relationship be severed, though even then the separation is less than easy: Cavalletto watching Rigaud in the Marshalsea automatically "resume[s] the attitude . . . in which he had sat before the same man in the deeper shade of another prison, one hot morning in Marseilles," and Pancks "recoil[s] in consternation" from his own shearing of Casby and then "fle[es] for a place of hiding, where he might lie sheltered from the consequences of his crime" (*LD*, 742, 803). While something like a normal ego could probably be extracted from the combined qualities of Casby/Pancks or Rigaud/Cavalletto, the fragmentation into opposed extremes eliminates any sense of wholeness or normality.

Even more intricately constructed than these paired units are the larger clusters of interconnected characters that together form group personalities or detailed explorations of a particular condition or trait. Repeatedly the narrative suggests, for instance, that those characters who make up what might be called the House of Clennam—Mrs. Clennam, Arthur, Jeremiah Flintwinch, Affery—are best imagined as a single, indissoluble entity. Flintwinch is the maleficent spirit of his immobilized mistress/partner, uttering her words and acting out her repressed desires; like the third side of a triangle, he "stand[s] between" (*LD*, 32) first Mr. and Mrs. Clennam, then Mrs. Clennam and Arthur, ensuring that the antagonists will neither reconcile nor separate altogether. Flora Finching, perspicacious as usual, describes Flintwinch "without the lightest boundary line of separation between his identity and Mrs. Clennam's" and conflates mother, son, and manservant into Clennam and Co., a messy "compound of man and woman, no limbs, wheels, rusty screw, grimness, and gaiters" (*LD*, 624). Affery too is incapable of imagining Flintwinch and Mrs. Clennam as separate beings and seems tied to both at the unconscious level: the line hanging beside Mrs. Clennam's hand activates a bell "within a foot of Mrs. Flintwinch's ear" and rouses her to action "before she [is] awake"; and Flintwinch haunts her ostensible dreams, where she is "completely under his influence" (*LD*, 41, 43). Her passivity and near thought-lessness—"I'd got something to do, without thinking, indeed!"—make her the perfect complement to "them two clever ones" and, as Arthur imagines, "the last thread wanting to the pattern" (*LD*, 38, 40) of the Clennam household.

While Arthur is the only member of the Clennam grouping whose autonomous personality might be considered "rounded," together they form a complex, highly nuanced study of the deformative effects of guilt—a study that could not plausibly be carried out within the boundaries of a single consciousness, even one of Raskolnikov-like dimensions. Each character's response to guilt acquires additional meaning and clarity when measured against the responses of the others. The eagerness of Arthur and Affery to acknowledge blame for uncommitted crimes is balanced by the complementary eagerness of Mrs. Clennam and Flintwinch to deny blame for crimes committed; the extent to which Mrs. Clennam's efforts are unsuccessful is in turn clarified by Flintwinch's easy, groundless self-exoneration. The strength of Arthur's desire to investigate the source of his remorse is at once highlighted and validated by Affery's self-elected ignorance. Such relationships both draw the Clennam characters together into a closely knit unit and undermine that unit with tensions and instabilities: like the building they inhabit, the structure formed by these figures seems always on the edge of collapse.

The characters grouped within the Casby household function comparably as an interdependent and mutually enlightening unit. The pairings of Casby/Pancks and Flora/Mr. F.'s Aunt fit together into a larger structure that dramatizes the dissolution of the linkage between surface and substance, as the Clennam characters dramatize the effects of guilt. Casby's deliberate, carefully controlled separation of appearance from personality contrasts with the more deep-seated, uncontrollable separation of Pancks; the latter's relatively stable self-division—stable enough at least for one side of his nature to identify and abuse the other—sheds light on the even less regulated separation between external and internal life in Flora; and she in turn highlights the utter mystery of Mr. F.'s Aunt, in whom the relations between external and internal meaning are altogether incomprehensible. Again, the complex presentation of psychological life lies not within but among a group of characters that the reader is invited repeatedly to understand collectively.

These group personalities generate yet another tension within Dickens's presentation of character. If, as George Levine claims, "Dickens's characters [typically] behave as though they had single, discoverable selves that constitute their essence" (a claim with which one might take issue), still the sense of stability created by these essential selves is counterbalanced by the larger, more unstable structures within which they operate.[18] Mrs. Clennam or Pancks may be fairly straightforward embodiments of guilt or split personality, but they are presented within contexts that show guilt and self-division to be highly complex conditions capable of assuming a variety of forms. Though in the novel the variety is divided among characters, the invitation to imagine these characters collectively implies, I think, that it might as easily be located within a single consciousness, were that consciousness to be glimpsed whole. But for Dickens, more than for most novelists, the belief seems to be that it cannot be glimpsed whole, so the sensible thing is to divide the complexity among a group of related fragments. In such a world, David Simpson notes, "one has to go the rounds from one individual to another in order to be able to piece together a complete image of the species."[19] Given this proclivity, it makes no more sense to define Dickens's presentation of guilt or any other quality on the basis of a single character than to define the personality of a protagonist in James or Eliot on the basis of a single scene.

Exemplified in this presentation of fragmented personality is the chief benefit of studying Victorian literature and culture through the works of Dickens: he manages to combine historical typicality—"Dickens was a man of his century," Kaplan claims, "There is no better representative"[20]—with an ability to embody the typical in forms of exceptional clarity and force. Thus the representative is defined and cast into relief through the originality of the ways it becomes expressed in Dickens's fiction. Here he is less noteworthy for his perception of fragmented or self-contradictory personality than for the extent to which that sense of personality shapes his presentation of character: if he believed little new or idiosyncratic about human consciousness, he managed to create a highly effective vehicle for the embodiment of those beliefs. Many, perhaps most Victorian writers and intellectuals understood personality in ways that bear some resemblance to Dickens's, but the work of very few was shaped by that understanding so pervasively and productively.

18. Levine is quoted from *Darwin*, 144.
19. Simpson, *Fetishism*, 42.
20. Kaplan, *Mesmerism*, 230.

Certainly the literary context within which Dickens's exploration of personality is situated includes many influences and analogues. "[He] learned from the Romantics," Kaplan observes, "that the mind was often complex and inconsistent, and that the outer signs that mind sought and created were sometimes perfect representations of the contradictions within the mind itself."[21] Blake's celebration of contrary states, at once inseparable and antagonistic; Keats's exploration of paradox, and especially the paradoxical symbiosis of pleasure and pain; Byron's self-tormented protagonists; Mary Shelley's externalization of the internal conflict between the civilized and the monstrous: all form a broad background out of which Dickens's conception of personality emerges. According to Kincaid, many of his best-known contemporaries "became more than a little uneasy with simple notions of an essentialised self. Presentation of a multiple self or of a hidden, unknown self are common" in Arnold and Browning, Tennyson and Meredith.[22] Arnold's description in *Empedocles on Etna* of the human tendency to become "prisoners of our consciousness," lost in "some fantastic maze/Forged by the imperious lonely thinking-power" (2.352, 375–76), suggests a concern with duality and self-deception comparable to that found in *Little Dorrit*. Tennyson's complaint in "The Two Voices" about his "divided will" (106) is reminiscent of Clennam's, and his dramatizations of psychological paralysis are as recurrent and powerful as Dickens's: both "Mariana," for instance, with its image of the isolated, frustrated woman, and "The Kraken," with its symbolic warning about the explosive consequences of repression, illuminate the characters of Mrs. Clennam and Miss Wade. The self-deluding fictions created by many of the speakers of Browning's dramatic monologues are as elaborate as those of Flora Finching and William Dorrit.

Among Victorian novelists the understanding of personality as multilayered, fluid, and potentially divided is reflected in formal developments and recurrent motifs too widely discussed to need much rehearsal here: the growing interiority of characterization, the rise of the developmental novel, and the prevalence of the doppelgänger, among other things, suggest how the mind came to be perceived and represented through the nineteenth century. Jane Eyre stands in for a whole class of characters when she lingers "before a looking-glass"

21. Ibid., 230.
22. Kincaid, "Performance," 13.

and "involuntarily explore[s] the depths it reveal[s]." In that "vision-ary hollow" all looks "colder and darker . . . than in reality."[23] Indeed, the terms in which Dickens's characters are both praised and criticized by his contemporaries, especially after 1850, are similarly revealing. John Forster condemns the widespread desire among reviewers to "have every character in a tale laid bare as on a psychological dissect-ing table"; Edwin Whipple distinguishes Dickens from other novelists of the time in that he "has no paradoxes . . . to push, no scientific view of human nature to sustain," while G. H. Lewes, as I noted earlier, misses the presence of anything "fluctuating and incalculable" in his representation of personality.[24] All write with an awareness that the powers of science are being brought increasingly to bear on the operations of the mind and struggling to define their mysterious complexities and inconsistencies—though they disagree about how these scientific efforts should be reflected in the depiction of fictional character.

As these allusions to dissecting tables, science, and psychology indi-cate, the lines between literary analyses of character and those of other disciplines were in the nineteenth century especially unclear. "One idiosyncracy of nineteenth-century England," writes Ann Colley, "is the extent to which . . . specialized studies [of medicine and psychol-ogy] ran over into the more popular journals and magazines reviewing the arts and the political scene"[25]—including some edited by Dickens himself. Unlike today, science did not automatically take precedence over imaginative writing as a means of access to truth, so that novelists "did not defer to the prestige of science," and "fiction had as strong

23. Charlotte Brontë, *Jane Eyre*, 46.
24. Forster and Whipple are quoted in Collins, ed., *Critical Heritage*, 292, 479. Lewes is quoted in George H. Ford and Lauriat Lane Jr., eds., *The Dickens Critics*, 65–66.
25. Ann C. Colley, *Tennyson and Madness*, 12. Ekbert Faas and Howard W. Fulweiler make the same point: "Reviewers [of literature]," Faas writes, " . . . could hardly be unaware of introspective psychology, mesmerism, and psycho-logical medicine, particularly since these were repeatedly discussed in the very journals for which they wrote." *Retreat into the Mind: Victorian Poetry and the Rise of Psychiatry*, 46. More recently Fulweiler has noted that "Many students of Victorian England have pointed to the intellectual intercourse between [*sic*] the eminent scientists, artists, politicians, and intellectuals, the common efforts to deal with common problems, often with intellectual frameworks or vocabularies that seem quite similar." " 'A Dismal Swamp': Darwin, Design, and Evolution in *Our Mutual Friend*," 72.

a claim as psychology to find order in the life of the passions."[26] In a way that may seem peculiar to contemporary readers, the ideas and specialized discourse of poetry and biology, philosophy and physics, were comprehensible and responsive to one another. The consistencies among them are both more numerous and more easily discernible. Not just literary representations of personality, but explorations in virtually every field show the nineteenth century to be what Colley and Ekbert Faas respectively call "an age overwhelmed by its sense of instability" and "an age . . . obsessed with the self and its ever-threatening disintegration."[27]

That neither "overwhelmed" nor "obsessed" is too strong a term is made clear by a number of developments in the nineteenth century that both influenced and reflected how the self was understood. Among the most revealing of these, especially for the student of Dickens, is the rise of mesmerism as both a scientific theory and a form of polite-society entertainment—an "odd blend," according to Taylor Stoehr, "of hard- and soft-headedness, on the one hand comprising some of the best physiological and psychological thinking of the century, and on the other producing examples of gullibility, self-deception, and charlatanism matched only by our own Madison Avenue." Mesmerism eventually moved in a variety of directions, but it rested fundamentally on the belief that

> there existed an invisible fluid, like electricity, that suffused the universe, the harnessing of which would provide valuable psychological and phys-iological benefits. Through special techniques of concentration, receptive individuals could be mesmerized . . . so that their normal state of con-sciousness was replaced by mesmeric trance in which they were able to have extraordinary knowledge about themselves and others through heightened contact with the mesmeric fluid. In such states of heightened consciousness, subjects were not limited by the normal restrictions of reason and physical perception.[28]

Though Anton Mesmer developed and popularized his theories in the 1780s, their influence initially was restricted to central Europe— where it was, indeed, powerful enough to inspire Schopenhauer to call animal magnetism "the most momentous discovery ever made."

26. Chase, *Eros and Psyche*, 3–4.
27. Colley, *Tennyson*, 10; Faas, *Retreat*, 40.
28. Taylor Stoehr, *Dickens: The Dreamer's Stance*, 272; Kaplan, *Dickens*, 182–83.

After Dr. John Elliotson performed a series of public mesmeric demonstrations at London University in 1838, however, fascination with the new science became widespread in Victorian England and persisted through the midcentury. Never without a hint of the illicit, mesmerism nonetheless interested even skeptical writers, philosophers, and scientists because, as Faas indicates, it offered at least some "possibility of subjecting . . . split consciousness to systematic analysis."[29]

Mesmerism found supporters, students, or curious followers in Elizabeth Barrett, Tennyson, Harriet Martineau, Arnold, Clough, and Thackeray. In 1855 Browning published "Mesmerism," a dramatic monologue in the voice of an animal magnetizer.[30] Dickens's interest in mesmerism, though, was the most intense and well-known among Victorian writers and has certainly been the most exhaustively documented. He attended one of Elliotson's original demonstrations and, in the 1840s, discovered himself to have mesmeric powers that he exercised on his wife, his friends, and, most notoriously and repeatedly, Augusta de la Rue, a married neighbor in Genoa. "I have watched Dr. Elliotson's experiments from the first," he wrote in 1842, and "after what I have seen with my own senses, I should be untrue to myself if I shrunk for a moment from saying that I am a believer, and that I became so against all my preconceived opinions and impressions."[31] There is no evidence that his belief in mesmerism or in his own mesmeric powers ever waned, and in fact mesmerism seems to play a more prominent role in *The Mystery of Edwin Drood* than in any of his earlier novels. John Jasper, distinguished by "a look of intentness and intensity" (*ED*, 9), is almost certainly a mesmerist, and there appears to be a magnetic connection as well between the twins Helena and Neville Landless.

Dickens's interest in mesmerism is tied to his representation of fictional character at the most fundamental level, since it provides a scientific basis for his perception of personality as fragmented and self-contradictory. "In mesmeric trance," Kaplan explains, "the subject was often like an actor, playing a number of roles, the single conscious personality split into multiple, seemingly disharmonious parts.

29. Faas, *Retreat*, 38, 40. See also Kaplan's discussions in *Mesmerism*, 3ff., and *Dickens*, 182–83.

30. See Faas, *Retreat*, 39.

31. Quoted in Kaplan, *Mesmerism*, 54. Dickens's experience with mesmerism is discussed in great detail throughout Kaplan's book and, more briefly, in his *Dickens*, 182–85.

In instances in which the subject in trance in Elliotson's experiments did not disintegrate into fragments, the self that emerged was often radically different from the conscious self, as if inhibitions and repressions had been lifted." Mesmeric patients "created second selves, projections," and "were often schizophrenic, divided in their behavioristic patterns." Among those most susceptible to mesmeric trance were those diagnosed with partial insanity.[32] Dickens, along with many of his contemporaries, may not have founded his beliefs about the internal life on mesmeric science, but clearly he discovered there reinforcement of those beliefs and a set of images and explanations through which to express them. No wonder, really, that mesmerism appealed to so many creative artists and thinkers: it seemed to provide experimental verification of deeply felt intuitions and fears about the potential disintegration of the self.

Slightly antecedent to the rise of mesmerism as a mental science was the even more widespread and influential rise of phrenology. That the two phenomena are connected is suggested by the fact that Elliotson, the chief English proponent of mesmerism, was also the founder in 1830 of the Phrenological Society. Like mesmerism, phrenology originated in central Europe in the late eighteenth century and was imported later into England as a combination of science and fad. Its founder was Franz-Josef Gall, who began with the relatively tame assertion that "some relationship existed between . . . the shape of the head and the powers of the intellect"; its most influential popularizer was Gall's pupil, Johann Caspar Spurzheim, who attempted not just to catalogue and measure the parts of the brain but also to apply phrenology "to problems of contemporary philosophy, religion, and social reform." Largely through the efforts of Spurzheim and the English phrenologist George Combe, the attempt to read character in cranial shape became for a time immensely popular in England and America: Harriet Martineau ranked Combe's "great phrenological treatise," *Constitution of Man Considered in Relation to External Objects* (1828), with *Pilgrim's Progress, Robinson Crusoe,* and the Bible,[33] and allusions to phrenology can be found in the works of Dickens, Thackeray, Surtees, Bulwer-Lytton, George Eliot, and, most insistently, the Brontës. Charlotte, sounding very much like Combe, describes

32. Kaplan, *Mesmerism,* 118–19; Colley, *Tennyson,* 21.

33. David de Giustino, *Conquest of the Mind: Phrenology and Victorian Social Thought,* 13, 15, 29.

Hiram Yorke in *Shirley* as lacking "the organ of Veneration—a great want, and which throws a man wrong on every point where veneration is required. Secondly, he was without the organ of Comparison—a deficiency which strips a man of sympathy; and, thirdly, he had too little of the organs of Benevolence and Ideality, which took the glory and softness from his nature."[34] Devotees in America included Poe, Emerson, and Melville, who were mildly curious, and Stowe and Whitman, who were passionately so. The breadth of interest in phrenology on both sides of the Atlantic indicates, according to Richard Altick, "how widely it was disseminated—and credited—in early Victorian years."[35]

Phrenology shares with mesmerism a sense of the mind as a collection of fragments, or an "aggregate . . . of parts" that may "not all develop at the same time nor to the same degree." Some of these parts within a single individual, in all likelihood, would come into conflict with others, generating complex internal tensions and relationships. Unlike mesmerism, however, phrenology is a science of "precision and confidence,"[36] impelled by the belief that the fragments of the mind are both measurable and clearly revealed through external appearance. This may be why it seemed reassuring to an age anxious about the disintegration of the self and why it did not appeal particularly to Dickens, who distrusted both precise estimates of character and easy extrapolations from external to internal life. While he was never contemptuously dismissive of phrenology—perhaps because he liked and respected Elliotson—his references to it tend to be skeptical and ironic, quite unlike his utterly serious treatment of mesmerism. In *Sketches by Boz*, for instance, he draws upon phrenology in a humorous reflection on door knockers:

> Some phrenologists affirm, that the agitation of a man's brain by different passions, produces corresponding developments in the form of his skull. Do not let us be understood as pushing our theory to the full length of asserting, that any alteration in a man's disposition would produce a visible effect on the feature of his knocker. Our position merely is, that in such a case, the magnetism which must exist between a man and his

34. Charlotte Brontë, *Shirley*, 34.

35. See Richard D. Altick, *Presence of the Present: Topics of the Day in the Victorian Novel*, 561–62n; John D. Davies, *Phrenology Fad and Science: A 19th-Century American Crusade*, 118–25; Stoehr, *Dreamer's Stance*, 271–24; Chase, *Eros and Psyche*, 54–58.

36. de Giustino, *Conquest*, 18, 23.

knocker, would induce the man to remove, and seek some knocker more congenial to his altered feelings. (*SB*, 41)

It should be noted that this fanciful reference to phrenology and magnetism was written several years prior to Dickens's conversion by the mesmeric demonstrations of Elliotson. By 1841 a French visitor to Dickens would report that "he seemed to be much preoccupied with certain physiological studies, his enquiring and subtle mind was clearly exercised by magnetism, the systems of Gall and Mesmer, everything relating to the phenomenal existence of man."[37] Dickens was himself phrenologized in America in 1842, and references to phrenology in later works including *Martin Chuzzlewit* and "The Lazy Tour of Two Idle Apprentices" (1857), while critical of obvious charlatanism, are not uniformly facetious.[38]

Mesmerism and phrenology are interesting to consider because they are so closely identified with the nineteenth century and directly alluded to in Dickens's own work. But other, more lasting and reputable developments of the time reveal as clearly an absorption with the instability and fragmentation of personality. Introspective psychology and psychological medicine have their roots in the nineteenth century, and the many attempts to define and institutionally treat insanity highlighted the vulnerability of the self to division or erosion. "Few Victorian autobiographies, lives, or, for that matter, collections of letters," Colley notes, "overlook their subjects' 'mental crises,'" and the essays of Macaulay, Carlyle, Newman, and Mill "rarely escape allusions to the tormented mind." Positivist philosophy, so influential around midcentury, proposed a model of the self as inevitably divided: for Ludwig Feuerbach, Levine summarizes, "the distinctively human begins with self-consciousness; and self-consciousness is self-fragmentation, the power of the self to make itself an object." Levine has indicated too how Darwinism fostered "a growing uncertainty about the notion of an 'essential' self," calling into question "all those aspects of human identity and experience that are traditionally regarded as uniquely human." Even physics, with its new emphasis on entropy and the inevitable dissolution of systems, undermined faith in the integrity of the self: if the inexorable movement in all things is

37. Quoted in Michael Hollington, "The Live Hieroglyphic: Physiologie and Physiognomy in *Martin Chuzzlewit*," 59.
38. See the discussions in Altick, *Presence*, 523–24, and Hollington, "Hieroglyphic," 59–61.

"from order to disorder, from concentrated to dissipated energy,"[39] what were the implications for the stability of the individual mind?

Against this background, Dickens's presentation of fragmented inner lives appears an understandable reflection of the deepest anxieties of his age—a different and in some ways more direct reflection than the "realistic" internal characterization of Eliot or James. The attempt by such writers to represent a whole, gradually changing personality is an attempt to deny or evade the threat of fragmentation, comparable to the many poems by Arnold that "glimpse and then quickly look away from an absorption or dissolution of self."[40] It connects directly with developments in psychology and psychiatry during the late nineteenth and early twentieth centuries and, more generally, with the view of many Victorians "that as the physical sciences were making the natural world comprehensible and bringing it under control, so the social sciences could make human experience comprehensible and bring *that* under control." Dickens, depending on one's perspective, either remains caught in an age prior to the rise of psychoanalysis or anticipates an age when the confident claims of psychoanalysis to provide an integrated picture of the mind would come to seem questionable—when, to cite Chase again, the tendency is "to conceive the personality not as an atomistic unit but as a play of complex and competing processes."[41] It is no surprise that Eliot was drawn primarily to phrenology and Dickens primarily to mesmerism.[42] Both disciplines imagine the mind as a collection of differing fragments, but whereas the former tries always to combine the fragments into a coherent, relatively stable whole, the latter imagines a state of ongoing self-division. One is a science of assembly, of fitting together the pieces to a single personality; the other is a science of uncovering the multiple, semiautonomous personalities existing within a single consciousness.

39. Faas, *Retreat*, 35–46; Colley, *Tennyson*, 10; George Levine, "By Knowledge Possessed: Darwin, Nature, and Victorian Narrative," 369; Levine, *Darwin*, 146, 159.

40. Kincaid, "Performance," 13. Levine identifies a belief in gradual change as a defining characteristic of realism and notes, "Dickens tended to find thoroughgoing gradualism inadequate. . . . His complex relation to this idea . . . suggests some of the limitations and contradictions within the realist project." *Darwin*, 16.

41. Levine, "Knowledge Possessed," 372; Chase, *Eros and Psyche*, 32.

42. Eliot wrote in 1855, "I never believed more profoundly than I do now that character is based on organization. I never had a higher appreciation than I have now of the services which phrenology has rendered towards the science of man." *The George Eliot Letters*, vol. 2, 210.

One calls to mind the dominant trends in realistic fiction and criticism, the other the characterization of Dickens.

The evolution of Dickens's representation of internal life parallels generally the evolution of his descriptive style, with a steady, if not wholly uninterrupted, progression toward greater self-consciousness and uncertainty about the reliability of comprehensive judgments. Characters with fragmented personalities, along with pairs or groups of interconnected personalities, appear in his work from the start, though the nature of the self-divisions tends to be more extreme in the later novels and the structuring of the group personalities more elaborate. Still, the split within Ralph Nickleby or Edith Dombey is nearly as stark as that within Tattycoram, and the grouping within the Cheeryble household a cruder (not to mention more chipper) version of the Casbys or Clennams. Sarah Gamp's creation of Mrs. Harris, her fictional second self, anticipates Nobody and the "poor little tiny woman" and is similarly based on a deep psychological need: when the existence of Mrs. Harris is questioned, "the shock of this blow was so violent and sudden, that Mrs. Gamp sat staring at nothing with uplifted eyes, and her mouth open as if she were gasping for breath" (*MC*, 756). What distinguishes the later from the earlier fiction-making is the extent to which it is acknowledged within *Little Dorrit* itself as a sign of repression and self-division.

Open references to dual consciousness can be found in many of Dickens's works beginning with *Oliver Twist*, which was being written when Dickens attended Elliotson's demonstrations and when, according to Kaplan, he "had already taken the subject [of mesmerism] into his creative consciousness."[43] Two nearly identical passages describe Oliver lingering between sleeping and waking and seem to dramatize Feuerbach's "power of the self to make itself an object":

> There is a drowsy state, between sleeping and waking, when you dream more in five minutes with your eyes half open, and yourself half conscious of everything that is passing around you, than you would in five nights with your eyes fast closed, and your senses wrapt in perfect unconsciousness. At such times, a mortal knows just enough of what his mind is doing, to form some glimmering conception of its mighty powers, its bounding from earth and spurning time and space, when freed from the restraint of its corporeal associate.

43. Kaplan, *Mesmerism*, 145.

There is a kind of sleep that steals upon us sometimes, which, while it holds the body prisoner, does not free the mind from a sense of things about it, and enable it to ramble at its pleasure. So far as an overpowering heaviness, a prostration of strength, and an utter inability to control our thoughts or power of motion, can be called sleep, this is it; and yet, we have a consciousness of all that is going on about us, and, if we dream at such a time, words which are really spoken, or sounds which really exist at the moment, accommodate themselves with surprising readiness to our visions. (*OT,* 58, 255)

This hypnagogic state combines two different forms of consciousness, the waking and the dreaming, and, more generally, fragments the mind into two portions, one of which seems aware of, even in awe of, the other. It calls into question the notion of the self as a single, indissoluble entity and raises the possibility of other, more debilitating varieties of self-division.

Precisely this form of dual consciousness is discussed by Dickens in 1851, in a letter to Dr. Thomas Stone, author of a piece on "Dreams" for *Household Words.* In our dreams, Dickens writes, "we all astonish ourselves by telling ourselves, in a dialogue with ourselves, the most astonishing and terrific secrets." Continually "some waking and reasoning faculty of the brain" endeavors as we dream "to correct our delusions."[44] Thus, asleep, the confrontation between opposed portions of the mind becomes more openly acknowledged than when awake, the struggle between rational and delusive impulses more overt. This struggle is not very different from, say, the one within William Dorrit between fiction and reality, the Father of the Marshalsea and the pathetic debtor, whose periodic uncovering leaves him embarrassed and disoriented. Clennam's reflections on Nobody, too, might be considered a waking version of this dream "dialogue with ourselves." That dual consciousness is not exclusively a characteristic of the sleeping mind is suggested by Dickens in his 1852 article, also for *Household Words,* on "Lying Awake." "Perhaps," he speculates, "with no scientific intention or invention, I was illustrating the theory

44. Charles Dickens, *The Letters of Charles Dickens,* vol. 6, 279. Among other things, Dickens's letter to Stone confirms his interest in nineteenth-century theories of psychology. "I have read something on the subject [of dreams]," he writes, "and have long observed it with the greatest attention and interest" (276). Warrington Winters examines Dickens's response to Stone at length in "Dickens and the Psychology of Dreams." Winters speculates that Dickens's contributions to Stone's essay on "Dreams" are so significant as to make the piece "in a sense a collaboration" (985).

of the Duality of the Brain; perhaps one part of my brain, being wakeful, sat up to watch the other part which was sleepy" (*UC,* 431).

This power of the mind to divide, observe, and enter into dialogue with itself was of sufficient interest to Dickens to force its way into virtually all of his novels, where descriptions of characters hovering between sleeping and waking, or delirium and rationality, are common. Through the productions of the 1840s runs a series of set-pieces depicting the peculiarities of dual consciousness: a feverish Dick Swiveller lying in a "waking slumber" under the care of the Marchioness (*OCS,* 474); Barnaby Rudge tormented by a guilt that "pursues him through his dreams, gnaws at the heart of all his fancied pleasures, robs the banquet of its taste, music of its sweetness, makes happiness itself unhappy, and yet is no bodily sensation, but a phantom without shape, or form, or visible presence" (*BR,* 471); Montague Tigg tossing in his own waking slumber in the terrifying presence of Jonas Chuzzlewit; Carker in hallucinatory flight from Dombey, with "contradiction pervad[ing] all his thoughts" (*DS,* 770). In later novels the dreams or deliriums of Esther Summerson and Affery Flintwinch, Jarvis Lorry and Pip, dramatize similar mental divisions.[45] Such scenes reflect, again, Dickens's tendency to make explicit at certain definitive moments impulses or strategies implicit throughout his fiction: the fragmentation of personality, like the uncertainty of language and perception, periodically becomes the subject of the narrative.

Nowhere is the fragmentation of personality more openly the subject of the narrative than in *The Mystery of Edwin Drood.* The novel's plot, of course, appears to turn around the frightening split within John Jasper and was, at least according to John Forster, to have culminated in a "review of the murderer's career by himself at the close, when its temptations were to be dwelt upon as if, not the culprit, but some other man, were the tempted."[46] Certainly one can find ample preparation for such an ending in the string of references throughout the novel to self-division and dual consciousness. "In some cases of drunkenness," the narrator observes near the start, "and in others

45. I am indebted to Winters's dated but informative article for the cataloguing of many of these references. See "Psychology of Dreams," 1000–1003.

46. John Forster, *The Life of Charles Dickens,* vol. 3, 463. While many have challenged the reliability of Forster's claim—indeed, a small industry has arisen to propose alternative endings—it remains the most plausible prediction of the novel's outcome.

of animal magnetism, there are two states of consciousness which never clash, but each of which pursues its separate course as though it were continuous instead of broken (thus, if I hide my watch when I am drunk, I must be drunk again before I can remember where)" (*ED*, 20). Among the novel's characters, Miss Twinkleton "has two distinct and separate phases of being" (*ED*, 20); Durdles, like so many others in Dickens, "often speaks of himself in the third person" (*ED*, 37); Neville Landless, in a rage, is "half-conscious" (*ED*, 77) of both his internal fury and his external surroundings; Mr. Grewgious describes the " 'true lover . . . as living at once a doubled life and a halved life' " (*ED*, 122) and, again, occasionally addresses himself in the third person; Rosa Bud "waver[s] in a divided state" between conflicting desires; and Jasper, above all, is caught in a never-ending struggle to remain "self-repressed" (*ED*, 223). Oliver Twist's moments of drowsy self-division have here become something approaching the general human condition.

Probably the best way to gauge the increasing complexity and self-consciousness of Dickens's internal characterization is to consider briefly the evolution of his protagonists, those "drably virtuous stick-figures" who have been the subject of so much derision (or, conspicuously, *not* the subject of so much laudatory criticism).[47] No critical sleight of hand can transform Edward Chester or Walter Gay into a compelling creation. From the beginning, however, Dickens's protagonists reflect in some measure his understanding of the self, and in the later novels especially they become the vehicles through which that understanding is most comprehensively displayed. In *Little Dorrit*, that is, as in *A Tale of Two Cities, Great Expectations, Our Mutual Friend*, and *The Mystery of Edwin Drood*, the self-divided consciousness is explored most extensively through a central male figure (or figures) who is both internally fragmented and a fragment contained within a larger collective consciousness.

Even among the relatively uncomplicated heroes of the early novels one can find signs of self-division and fragmentation. Of the novels prior to *David Copperfield*, only *Nicholas Nickleby* and *Martin Chuzzlewit* actually include fairly traditional, continuously observed male protagonists, and even Nicholas and Martin disappear for long stretches when the focus shifts to characters such as Kate Nickleby

47. Beth F. Herst, *The Dickens Hero: Selfhood and Alienation in the Dickens World,* 1.

and Tom Pinch. Both are internally divided along pretty obvious lines, Nicholas between his passivity and goodness on the one hand and his violent temper on the other, Martin between his natural kindness and thoughtless conceit. Nicholas especially seems marked by some form of dual consciousness: he warns Squeers not to " 'raise the devil in me,' " suggesting the existence of a second, uncontrollable self, and, once that self takes control, typically becomes "conscious of nothing but his fury" (*NN*, 155, 417), losing all awareness of his more rational, ethical side. Not surprisingly, the conflicts within both characters are contained safely within a process of maturation that allows them to be resolved or outgrown.

More interesting is the grouping around these early protagonists of other characters who act as counterparts or alter egos, commenting on and clarifying their personalities. Such groupings might be considered preliminary versions of the extensive personality clusters seen in the later novels. Nicholas Nickleby and Smike are first cousins of similar age and, to some extent, with similar desires, allowing the latter to serve clearly as a victimized "surrogate for his more fortunate cousin."[48] "In Smike on the one hand and Nicholas on the other," Steven Marcus notes, "a life such as Oliver Twist's is divided into its principle components: Oliver's protected character and destiny, which Dickens gives to Nicholas, and Oliver's terrible experiences, which he continues to represent in Smike."[49] Despite Nicholas's early promise to Smike that " 'the world shall deal by you as it does by me, till one or both of us shall quit it for a better,' " they are from beginning to end dealt with utterly differently, with "all the spleen and ill-humour that could not be vented on Nicholas . . . unceasingly bestowed" upon Smike (*NN*, 159, 143). Not just Nicholas's good fortune, but his self-assertiveness, intolerance of evil, and penchant for violence are cast into relief by the contrasting example of his cousin; certainly the precise nature of his inactivity is defined in comparison to Smike's more pathetic yet somehow more noble passivity.

The pattern is repeated more elaborately in *Martin Chuzzlewit*, where Martin is explored through comparison to Tom Pinch and, less directly, John Westlock and Mark Tapley, all of whom ring changes on

48. Ibid., 15. Badri Raina discusses the "assiduity of detail with which Dickens consolidates [the] surrogate structure" of Nicholas and Smike. See *Dickens and the Dialectic of Growth*, 40–41.

49. Marcus, *Pickwick*, 121.

his defining characteristics. "In terms of future technique," writes Beth Herst, "the proliferation of these figures, variations on young Martin himself, is an important development of Nicholas's doubling by Smike. It is a method Dickens will employ with increasing sophistication to enhance the depiction of the hero's experience."[50] More fundamentally, as I have been suggesting, such variations complicate the depiction of personality itself by expanding traits beyond the boundaries of individual characters and by causing every trait to call quickly to mind its opposites, alternatives, and extreme forms. *Barnaby Rudge,* though lacking a single, central hero, provides a similar cluster of characters linked through comparison and contrast: the personal and political desires of Edward Chester and Joe Willet, representatives of sanity and social order, are parodied and perverted by those of the bestial Hugh, the mad Barnaby, and the disgruntled Sim Tappertit.

— What distinguishes *David Copperfield* from these earlier novels is not David's distorted mirroring by Steerforth and Uriah Heep but the extent to which David himself seems aware of and troubled by his own fragmentation. Nicholas and Martin may be parts of a larger whole but are oblivious to, and thus undisturbed by, their incompleteness; increasingly in the later novels the protagonists appear to recognize and indeed to create some of their own second selves. Whereas Nicholas's reaction to Smike is in no way conditioned by their status as counterparts, the intensity of David's attraction to Steerforth and repulsion by Heep relates clearly to his recognition, albeit mostly unconscious, that they act out alternative versions of his own desires. Heep in particular, to whom David is paradoxically "attracted . . . in very repulsion," seems born out of the protagonist's own psyche: "He seemed to swell and grow before my eyes; the room seemed full of the echoes of his voice; and the strange feeling . . . that all this had occurred before, and that I knew what he was going to say next, took possession of me." Later David confesses that Heep "knew me better than I knew myself" (*DC,* 383, 381, 621). As is suggested by his many different names—Daisy and Doady, Trotwood and Copperfield, Master and Mister—David is also more radically self-divided than any previous Dickens hero. His "love for Agnes," Kucich argues, "as well

---

50. Herst, *Dickens Hero,* 26. See also Welsh's discussion of the Cain/Abel motif in Dickens in *City of Dickens,* 130–37, and Harry Stone's discussion of the double in *Dickens and the Invisible World: Fairy Tale, Fantasy, and Novel-Making,* 302–3.

as his refusal to act on it are both to his credit, according to his own evaluation, and his exemplary status as a character seems to depend on his being able to entertain both impulses at once. Rather than leading to frustration and inhibition, divided impulses produce an enigmatic and potent doubleness."[51] Unlike in Dickens's earlier novels, neither side of David's conflict, neither passion nor repression, is explicitly rejected here, nor is either eventually outgrown.

Arthur Clennam and Pip are David Copperfield's most direct descendants, though each is even more openly self-divided and more conscious of his self-division. Clennam's conflict between desire and repression, along with his status as a fragment within a group personality, has already been discussed. Where David's surrogate names are invented by others, Clennam creates "Nobody" himself. His version of Uriah Heep is Rigaud, who, as several critics have pointed out, acts mysteriously as Clennam's dark alter ego, a relationship of which both characters seem dimly aware. "If Rigaud is Clennam's double," Alexander Welsh speculates, "the plot of Little Dorrit makes a little more sense," since Rigaud "behaves as if he obeyed motives that logically belong to the hero"[52]—particularly in his tormenting of Flintwinch and Mrs. Clennam. As David recoils from Heep, so Clennam responds with overwhelming distaste to the mere sight of Rigaud; this time, however, even more maddeningly, the doppelgänger flaunts his own role, deliberately echoing Clennams's speech, calling him "fellow jail-bird" and "brother-bird," and proclaiming that the two are virtually "all alike" (LD, 742, 745). He too seems to know the protagonist better than he knows himself.

=-1 Great Expectations, a more tightly focused novel than David Copperfield or Little Dorrit, seems to concentrate its presentation of fragmentation and self-conflict into a number of exceptionally vivid examples: Wemmick, for instance, is a more starkly and self-consciously divided version of Pancks, and Estella an utterly unrepentant creator of a safely distanced second self (" 'You speak of yourself,' " Pip admonishes her, " 'as if you were some one else' " [GE, 252]). So, not surprisingly, Pip's divided personality is conveniently characterized by Herbert Pocket, who calls him " 'a good fellow, with impetuosity and hesitation, boldness and diffidence, action

51. Kucich, Repression, 227.
52. Welsh, City of Dickens, 135. See also Showalter, "Guilt," 32 and Stoehr, Dreamer's Stance, 178.

and dreaming, curiously mixed in him' " (*GE*, 234). Because his reaction to nearly every character and situation in the novel is ambivalent or self-contradictory, his emotional life remains perpetually in what Kucich terms a "delicate stat[e] of internal tension." Seen from this perspective, the revised, "happier" ending to the novel may be the more appropriate one, since it shows Pip's last words to Biddy—" 'that poor dream, as I once used to call it, has all gone by, Biddy, all gone by!' " (*GE*, 457)—to be followed by his final, blatantly self-contradictory return to Satis House. Here Orlick plays, even more openly than Heep or Rigaud, the role of "dark shadow and aggressive extension"[53]— and, one might add, psychoanalytic critic, as he provides his own reading of Pip's repressed desires: " 'It was you as did for your shrew sister. . . . I tell you it was your doing—I tell you it was done through you' " (*GE*, 404).

The remaining late novels present not single, fragmented protagonists but protagonist clusters of increasing complexity. From its title onward, Herst indicates, *A Tale of Two Cities* "declares itself to be constructed on a principle of polarity,"[54] a principle whose most obvious manifestation (aside from the juxtaposition of London and Paris) is the resemblance/opposition of Charles Darnay and Sydney Carton. Though this pairing is rather conventional and clear-cut by the standards of Dickens's mature fiction, it does serve as an interesting externalization of the internal conflicts seen in the contemporaneous Clennam and Pip. For most of the novel, until the melodramatic events at the conclusion, Darnay and Carton embody the two sides of Pip as defined by Herbert Pocket, the one being marked by "impetuosity, . . . boldness, . . . and action," the other by "hesitation, . . . diffidence, . . . and dreaming." Each, moreover, is himself self-divided: Carton conceals (except before Lucie Manette) his better nature beneath a mask of cynical indifference, while Darnay struggles between his identities as English citizen and French aristocrat.

In *Our Mutual Friend* the methods of the previous three novels are carried further. John Harmon, Eugene Wrayburn, and Bradley Headstone present the reader with a triumvirate of divided, intricately

---

53. Kucich, *Repression*, 252; Stone, *Invisible World*, 305. Stone's is one of many readings of Orlick as Pip's double, the most influential of which has been Julian Moynahan's in "The Hero's Guilt: The Case of *Great Expectations*." See also Herst, *Dickens Hero*, 127–28.

54. Herst, *Dickens Hero*, 145.

connected characters who dramatize the disintegration of the stable, integrated self.[55] Each is radically fragmented: Harmon's "alienation from himself" is signaled by a succession of different names that, unlike David Copperfield's, are self-elected; Wrayburn, like Sydney Carton, is "divided between a true self and an assumed/imposed identity which betrays it"; and Headstone, as John Lucas observes, "is the most pitiable and horrifying case of a split identity" in a novel filled with such cases.[56] The three cohere together as the novel's central interest, embodying, interchanging, and testing the potential of a limited set of recurrent characteristics. More telling than the fairly obvious plot parallels—both Harmon and Wrayburn nearly drown, both Harmon and Headstone adopt disguises, both Headstone and Wrayburn love Lizzie Hexam—are the connections established in Dickens's almost obsessively reiterative descriptive prose. Initially Harmon is "constrained, reserved, diffident, troubled," with "something repressed" in his manner, and later Bella Wilfer observes that " 'you [Harmon] repress yourself, and force yourself, to act a passive part' " (*OMF*, 38, 96, 521). Headstone, even more than Harmon, repeatedly shows signs of "suppression," "repression," and "restraint" and impresses observers less perceptive than Bella with his painfully "constrained manner" (*OMF*, 217, 387, 546, 217). Wrayburn too is "ill at ease with himself," passive (" 'If there is a word in the dictionary that I abominate, it is energy' "), and trapped in a false role ("his part was played out for the evening, and . . . he came off the stage" [*OMF*, 691, 20, 407]). Harmon, ostensibly the hero, contains elements of dissatisfaction and repression that are dramatized more vividly in Wrayburn and Headstone, while they are extreme characters whose dominant traits are incorporated into a broader, more moderate personality in Harmon. The miraculous, happily resolved story of the one is supported and deepened by the more somber, intertwined stories of the others. In a more elaborate version of the relationship between Tattycoram and Miss Wade, Wrayburn and Headstone illustrate the potential directions a nature such as Harmon's might take.

55. "All of the characters [in *Our Mutual Friend*] are divided . . . and thus often mysterious. . . . Almost all the characters in the novel lead double lives." Fulweiler, "Dismal Swamp," 67.

56. Connor, *Charles Dickens*, 152; Herst, *Dickens Hero*, 151; Lucas, *Melancholy Man*, 327.

The Mystery of Edwin Drood continues the trends established in
A Tale of Two Cities and *Our Mutual Friend*. Again the protagonist's role is distributed among more than one character, and more
than ever before the focus is predominantly on inchoate, self-divided
personalities. Had the novel continued, the conventional Lieutenant
Tartar might well have assumed a larger role, but as it stands John
Jasper, Edwin Drood, and Neville Landless form a troubled, repressed
triptych reminiscent of Harmon, Wrayburn, and Headstone. Their
gradual convergence in the chapter "When Shall These Three Meet
Again?" seems an almost inevitable coming together of three related
parts of a single whole and precipitates the novel's central event. Jasper
especially, as many commentators have pointed out, is Dickens's most
open presentation of the dual personality. "Jasper's predicament,"
Herst writes, is that "he has divided himself into two halves that can
never make a whole. No single 'normal' identity can unite the self he
has dissevered so radically."[57] Among the several scenes emblematic
of his fragmentation is the early one in which his "breathing seems to
have stopped" until he "becom[es] a breathing man again without the
smallest stage of transition between the two extreme states" (*ED*, 15).
All Dickens's suppressed, self-contradictory, unstable characters seem
to devolve finally into the frightening choirmaster who, if John Forster
is to be believed, was to be revealed as his ultimate creator of surrogate
second selves. The potential chaos implicit in so many Dickensian
personalities becomes in the end explicit and destructive.

Let me reiterate finally my argument and some of its general implications. As most readers have surely recognized, Dickens's characters
rarely create the (inevitably false) impression of psychological wholeness created by the central figures of the nineteenth-century realists:
few would call any of his characters, as Geoffrey Tillotson calls Charlotte Brontë's Lucy Snowe, "among the most fully realised persons in
fiction," and few would dispute David Simpson's claim that "Dickens
is not for the most part writing the kind of novel in which the complex
analysis of what [Henry] James calls 'character' plays a large part."[58]

---

57. Herst, *Dickens Hero*, 176. Not the first but easily the most influential analysis of Jasper's self-division is Edmund Wilson's in "Dickens: The Two Scrooges."
"John Jasper," he writes, "has then 'two states of consciousness'; he is, in short,
what we have come to call a dual personality." See *The Wound and the Bow:
Seven Studies in Literature*, 92.
58. Geoffrey Tillotson, Introduction to *Villette*, xiv; Simpson, *Fetishism*, 40.

He is, however, writing novels in which complex analysis of a slightly different sort takes place—not of a single, rounded personality, but of personality itself as distributed among a collection of fragmented and fragmentary characters. If the self-divisions, doublings, and collective consciousnesses he presents do not suggest the way a single mind habitually operates, they do suggest the multiplicity of ways the mind in general may operate under different circumstances and conditions. They suggest the range, diversity, and elusiveness of consciousness, more than its typical nature.

Character in what one might call, for convenience, the Jamesian sense, may be considered an attempt to approximate the way I, for instance, perceive my own consciousness, as something "full, rich, universally prehensile." Of this James himself was wholly aware, writing that "the fictive hero successfully appeals to us only as an eminent instance, as eminent as we like, of our own conscious kind."[59] The success of such characterization depends upon the extent to which it reminds me of myself, less in substance than in manner of thought. Character in the Dickensian sense may be considered an attempt to approximate the way I perceive the consciousness of every other being, as a mystery to be unraveled through fragmentary evidence, with some parts exaggerated and others omitted altogether. Its success depends upon the extent to which it reminds me of that challenging process of understanding. While it may be true that Tattycoram's personality seems nowhere near as complex as my own, it is equally true that my perception of, say, Isabel Archer in no way resembles my perception of the personality of anyone I know. The two are attempts to represent character from different, almost opposed perspectives, and the mistake, made in so much novel-criticism, lies in applying the same set of criteria to both.

59. James, *Theory of Fiction*, 155, 191.

5

"So Exactly Alike, and So Completely One"

Twins, Mirrors, and Shadows

MILDRED NEWCOMB has written recently that the distinctiveness of Dickens "lies first in his image-making mind. His figurative images develop into patterns and enlarge into allegories that encompass the extended meaning of his insights." This is anything but a universally accepted judgment: others such as John Carey have criticized the lack of coherence or consistency in Dickens's imagery, and few have gone so far as to consider him an allegorist in the accepted sense.[1] Neither would I, though I would agree that he possesses to an extraordinary degree the ability to encapsulate his ideas and insights into memorable and evocative images. Not always is the meaning of these images sharply defined, but that may be precisely why they compel attention: their placement and power suggest deep significance, but the text provides little indication of what that significance might be, or, equally often, it provides too much indication, implying competing or incompatible meanings. These are the sorts of teasing, ambiguous images about which articles get written.

Many of the best-known images in Dickens, such as the fog in *Bleak House,* the prison in *Little Dorrit,* and the dust heap in *Our Mutual Friend,* are too dominant to be merely teasing, yet they manage to become the focal point of significance in a particular novel without having a single definitive meaning. Instead they resonate throughout the text, seeming to lie at the center of every important description and conversation. Other images reappear throughout his fiction without dominating any single work and express ongoing ways in which he understands the world. Newcomb, for instance, identifies images such as the flowing river and the stagnant marsh as running through

1. Newcomb, *Imagined World,* 4; John Carey, *Here Comes Dickens: The Imagination of a Novelist,* 129–30.

virtually all of Dickens's novels and constituting a kind of recurrent pictorial vocabulary.[2] Not surprisingly, therefore, his understanding of character as contradictory and self-divided, central to his work nearly from the start, finds periodic expression in images of doubleness, duplication, and inversion—twins and mirrors, shadows and sleepers—that become in the later novels dizzyingly complex.

Among the most potent of such images in *Little Dorrit* is the early juxtaposition of Jeremiah Flintwinch and a nameless Double whose identity as his twin brother Ephraim is revealed only hundreds of pages later:

> Mr. Flintwinch awake, was watching Mr. Flintwinch asleep. He sat on one side of a small table, looking keenly at himself on the other side with his chin sunk on his breast, snoring. The waking Flintwinch had his full front face presented to his wife; the sleeping Flintwinch was in profile. The waking Flintwinch was the old original; the sleeping Flintwinch was the double. Just as she might have distinguished between a tangible object and its reflection in a glass, Affery made out this difference with her head going round and round. (*LD*, 41–42)

Here Flintwinch's fragmented personality is given physical form through a mysterious tableau of doubleness and opposition narrated from the perspective of his ostensibly "dreaming" wife. Already in the novel his personality has been described as divided between "natural acerbity and energy" and "habitual repression" (*LD*, 37); now the two sides of Flintwinch appear to have taken on independent existences in the waking and sleeping figures. The notion that "together [the two characters] are one personality"[3] is soon strengthened when Double awakens and proves to be passive, quiet, and careful, whereas Original is marked by "impatience" and "vehement energy" (*LD*, 42). Ephraim, it turns out, is, like many Dickensian doubles, both the image and the inverse of his original, matching Jeremiah's wickedness but exchanging his intensity and cleverness for laziness and incompetence. His former occupation as "lunatic-keeper" (*LD*, 783) accords nicely with his brother's role as guardian of the Clennam household.

The meeting of the Flintwinches to exchange secret documents makes literal and external the internal dream experience described by Dickens in his letter to Thomas Stone: "we all astonish ourselves by telling ourselves, in a dialogue with ourselves, the most astonishing

---

2. Newcomb, *Imagined World*, 6ff.
3. Kaplan, *Mesmerism*, 121.

and terrific secrets."[4] That the meeting takes place within Affery's "dream," with an air of unreality, only reinforces the connection. It recalls too the descriptions of one "waking" portion of the brain observing a second "sleeping" portion found most notably in *Oliver Twist* and the essay "Lying Awake." The description of "Mr. Flintwinch awake . . . watching Mr. Flintwinch asleep" echoes almost verbatim the words of "Lying Awake" ("one part of my brain, being wakeful, sat up to watch the other part which was sleepy" [*UC*, 431]), and the inexplicable enmity of the waking toward the sleeping Flintwinch ("He looked about him for an offensive weapon, and . . . lunged at the sleeper as though he would have run him through the body" [*LD*, 427]) may be understood as the denial by the rational of the dreaming mind. And the scene makes explicit the connections among three of Dickens's most recurrent images of the fragmented or dual personality: the sleeper, the double, and the "reflection in a glass." Altogether few episodes in *Little Dorrit* are both so extraneous to its plot and so expressive of its meaning.

Duplicate Flintwinches might be expected in a novel where, as Susan K. Gillman and Robert L. Patten have observed, the act of doubling is so pervasive that "the world itself seems twinned."[5] As the discussion in chapter 4 has suggested, nearly every character in *Little Dorrit* is caught in one or more relationships with alter egos, surrogates, or psychological complements: Clennam creates Nobody and is paralleled by Rigaud, who in turn forms a symbiotic pair with Cavalletto; Little Dorrit creates the tiny woman and is shadowed and enlarged by Maggy; for Tattycoram there are Pet Meagles and Miss Wade, for Flora, Mr. F's Aunt, for Casby, Pancks, and so it goes throughout the novel. The literal Flintwinch twins concretize these many figurative doublings, as does the second set of identical siblings in the novel, Pet and her dead twin sister, Lillie. Indeed, despite the fact that one happens no longer to be alive, the Meagles twins form an even more overt psychological unit than do the Flintwinch twins and embody even more clearly the fragmentation of personality. " 'Pet and her baby sister,' " Mr. Meagles recollects,

> were so exactly alike, and so completely one, that in our thoughts we have never been able to separate them since. It would be of no use to tell us that

4. Dickens, *Letters*, vol. 6, 279.
5. Gillman and Patten, "Doubles," 446.

our dead child was a mere infant. We have changed that child according to the changes in the child spared to us, and always with us. As Pet has grown, that child has grown; as Pet became more sensible and womanly, her sister has become more sensible and womanly, by just the same degrees. It would be as hard to convince me that if I was to pass into the other world to-morrow, I should not, through the mercy of God, be received there by a daughter, just like Pet, as to persuade me that Pet herself is not a reality at my side. (*LD,* 19)

For a dead person, this lost twin plays a surprisingly lively role in the novel. The bizarre insistence of the Meagleses on keeping her "alive" explains, in part, the unfinished quality of Pet's personality and her complicated mixture of guilt and resentment—as Fred Kaplan puts it, "Pet should have been given the opportunity to have had a lost sister."[6] Lillie is yet another surrogate for Tattycoram, who was, in effect, acquired to take her place without being given any legitimate opportunity to do so. And this other Meagles daughter might be considered the bride of Nobody, the "other" Arthur Clennam: " 'I feel,' " Mr. Meagles tells Clennam after Pet's betrothal and shortly before "Nobody's Disappearance," " 'as if you had loved my dead child very tenderly, and had lost her when she was like what Pet is now' " (*LD,* 331, 337).

Characters in *Little Dorrit* not paired with identical twins are haunted in other ways by inversions, duplications, or representations of their own figures. At least eight are described as literally or figuratively confronting images of themselves in mirrors, and often the mirror image is treated as a second, separate self: Fanny Dorrit "protest[s] to her looking-glass" about the behavior of her sister and "angrily [tells] her looking-glass" that she desires no sisterly forgiveness (*LD,* 588). Mrs. Clennam and Flintwinch, two fragments within a larger whole, are pictured as mirror images of one another: "she sat with her eyes fastened on the ground, and a certain air upon her of resolute waiting; . . . exactly the self-same expression was reflected in Mr. Flintwinch, standing at a little distance from her chair, with his eyes also on the ground, and his right-hand softly rubbing his chin" (*LD,* 628). The separation between the originals and the reflections in the novel is emphasized by the fact that many of the mirrors are murky or dimmed, providing unclear or distorted images: one is "meagre," another is "sullied," still another "seemed to hold in magic preservation

---

6. Kaplan, *Mesmerism,* 125.

all the fogs and bad weather it had ever reflected" (*LD*, 54, 124, 327). The mirror image, like the alternate self created by Arthur Clennam or the "second nature" of Flintwinch (*LD*, 37), is both familiar and alien, dependent upon yet mysteriously independent of the original.

Also simultaneously dependent and independent are images embodied in the shadow and the painted portrait, both of which are, as I have already indicated, extremely prevalent in *Little Dorrit*. Shadows are so pervasive and so deeply significant in the novel as to make identification of a single meaning almost impossible,[7] but among other things they serve as a further reminder of self-division—particularly in Little Dorrit's story of the Princess and in the Clennam household, where the "shadows of the two clever ones" (*LD*, 180) are glimpsed often enough almost to become independent beings. The recurrence of painted portraits in the novel has been less frequently remarked upon, though, as Martin Meisel has argued, this is probably the work containing Dickens's most sustained presentation and criticism of visual art.[8] The list of characters depicted in paintings or described via painting metaphors is strikingly long and includes Clennam's father, Tite Barnacle, Mr. Casby, Pet and Lillie Meagles, Rigaud, William, Frederick, and Amy Dorrit, Pancks, and Mr. Merdle. Typically the reference to painting conveys some sense of the mixture of accuracy and unreliability in the represented image: Casby, for instance, is "disguised" in his portrait, and Little Dorrit is "not quite convinced [she] should have known" her father from his painted likeness (*LD*, 145, 556). The portrait too is at best a "sullied" mirror. It can also be a powerful vehicle of self-alienation, as when William Dorrit observes, with existential discomfort, his daughter ministering to his brother: "Allowing for the great difference in the still-life of the picture, the figures were much the same as of old; his brother being sufficiently like himself to represent himself, for a moment, in the composition" (*LD*, 638).

These various images conjoin in what may be the most multilayered representation of doubling and inversion in Dickens, a resonant scene in Mr. Meagles's "own snug room":

7. Elaine Showalter, for instance, sees the shadow as an embodiment of the "omniscient narrator," the "secret self," and the "protective imagination," in "Guilt," 21; and J. Hillis Miller notes that "[the shadow] appears . . . in connection with almost all the characters" in the novel. See *World*, 229.

8. Meisel, *Realizations*, 303.

Clennam's eyes had strayed to a natural picture on the wall, of two
pretty little girls with their arms entwined. "Yes, Clennam," said Mr.
Meagles in a lower voice. "There they both are. It was taken some seventeen
years ago. As I often say to Mother, they were babies then."

"Their names?" said Arthur.

"Ah, to be sure! You have never heard any name but Pet. Pet's name is
Minnie; her sister's Lillie."

"Should you have known, Mr. Clennam, that one was meant for me?"
asked Pet herself, now standing in the doorway.

"I might have thought that both of them were meant for you, both are
still so like you. Indeed," said Clennam, glancing from the fair original to
the picture and back, "I cannot even now say which is not your portrait."

"D'ye hear that, Mother?" cried Mr. Meagles to his wife, who had
followed her daughter, "It's always the same, Clennam; nobody can decide.
The child to your left is Pet."

The picture happened to be near a looking-glass. As Arthur looked at
it again, he saw, by the reflection of the mirror, Tattycoram stop in passing
outside the door, listen to what was going on, and pass away with an
angry and contemptuous frown upon her face that changed its beauty into
ugliness. (*LD*, 193–94)

The doubling here—the sense of simultaneous separation and connection, difference and similarity—is at least five- or sixfold. The
"entwined" twins in the picture are mirror images of one another,
and in a larger sense the picture itself is an image or representation of reality (though a potentially unreliable one, as the novel has
already suggested). Pet is juxtaposed too with her own infant self,
a telling comparison in a story filled with contrasts between older
and younger identities. Clennam's ambiguously circuitous language—
"I cannot even now say which is not your portrait"—reinforces the
uncertainty of the connection between original and duplication. The
looking glass of course mirrors reality as well, and more specifically
it captures the altering image of Tattycoram, who is herself an imperfect re-creation of the departed Lillie. Tattycoram's own internal
division is recalled in her instantaneous transformation from "beauty"
to "ugliness" (as Clennam's is more subtly recalled by Mr. Meagles's
allusion to "nobody"). The fact that both Pet and Tattycoram are
"framed" in the doorway, finally, draws attention both to their own
uneasy relationship and to the implied comparison between these
living images and the two framed images on the wall.

Gillman and Patten, while noting the universality of doubling in
Little Dorrit, conclude curiously that "there are no explanations for
why this should be so." Precisely such an explanation is what I have

been trying thus far to provide. The novel may not be "about" doubling in the narrow sense that it is about varieties of imprisonment, but it presents in especially concentrated form Dickens's ongoing concern with dual or fragmented selves, and that concern is embodied often in images of the double. Perhaps if one assumes, as do Gillman and Patten, that "Dickens explores the ramifications of doubleness from a base that seems confident about individual identity,"[9] then the prevalence of the image appears mysterious, but my contention is that such confidence is, especially in Dickens's later novels, conspicuously absent. The elusiveness of character suggested by his uncertain descriptive language and partially glimpsed personalities is suggested as well by the proliferation of figures who are, like Minnie and Lillie Meagles, nearly impossible to tell apart.

Robert Garis has written that Dickens's "grasp on the whole Meagles family and what they represent is always uncertain and often distinctly inept." Significantly, he has also written that "none of [Dickens's] symbols is the vehicle for complex meaning like Chekhov's cherry orchard."[10] It may be precisely because Garis misses the complex symbolic ramifications of scenes such as the one in Mr. Meagles's room that he mistakes uncertainty for ineptness. As the images in that scene make clear, the uncertainty here lies not in Dickens's control of his material but in his doubts about the stability and comprehensibility of identity; and the contradictions and blurrings in the presentation of Pet and Tattycoram especially reflect not inept technique but a technique responsive to the view of internal character that informs much of Dickens's work. The problem is not that Dickens fails to grasp his subject, but that he is writing about a subject which, in his view, can never entirely be grasped.

Noteworthy examples of the imagery of self-division occur even in Dickens's early novels. *Nicholas Nickleby*'s Cheeryble brothers, however, his first set of identical twins, are not among them: Kaplan has described them aptly as being "like an identical blob of protoplasm, split into indistinguishable extensions. . . . There are no parts to the Cheeryble twins' unity, no depths of opposing and complementary forces."[11] Dickens may have felt the need for two Cheerybles to

9. Gillman and Patten, "Doubles," 446, 441.
10. Garis, *Dickens Theatre*, 122.
11. Kaplan, *Mesmerism*, 120.

balance as agents of goodness against the horde of nasty characters in the novel, but he does nothing here with the potential tension between separate yet identical beings. The Cheerybles are neither problematically entwined like the Meagles twins nor temperamentally opposed like the Flintwinches. They are remarkable chiefly as an early if undeveloped indication of Dickens's interest in the condition of identicality.

Much more suggestive are the images and descriptive set-pieces in *Barnaby Rudge,* a novel dominated on a number of levels by violent oppositions and contradictions that are, according to Steven Marcus, left finally "without resolution."[12] Perhaps more than in any other Dickens novel prior to *Little Dorrit,* one is left here with a world whose antagonistic forces have been quieted but not reconciled. The "Riots of 'Eighty' " are quelled, forcefully, but the imbalances responsible for them remain embedded in the organization of society; fathers cease to trouble sons, but only through the oblivion of madness or death. Clearly the implication is that certain kinds of social and personal conflict are inevitable and irreconcilable, ending periodically not with agreement but with the triumph, destruction, or utter exhaustion of one or the other antagonist.

The inevitability of conflict is embedded in *Barnaby Rudge* in the descriptions of characters, who tend to be presented in opposed pairs, as if any given set of physical traits automatically elicits a contradictory set. Emma Haredale and Dolly Varden are introduced in a clichéd counterpoint, with Emma "so fair, and Dolly so rosy, and Emma so delicately shaped, and Dolly so plump" (*BR,* 155); Gabriel Vardon and the elder Barnaby Rudge enter the novel after the observation that "two men more powerfully contrasted never opposed each other face to face" (*BR,* 20); Geoffrey Haredale and John Chester are physically "as unlike and far removed from each other as two men could well be" (*BR,* 90). The definitive grouping in the novel is of two characters locked, like Vardon and Rudge, face to face, each critically eyeing a figure to whom he is both painfully joined and energetically opposed.

Given the frequency with which characters in this novel stare at inverted versions of themselves, it is unsurprising that mirrors seem to be everywhere. *Barnaby Rudge* is not the first work in which Dickens makes use of the mirror to suggest dual or divided identity—Quilp, for

---

12. Marcus, *Pickwick,* 175. James Kincaid has noted too that *Barnaby Rudge* is "a novel based on reversal." See *Rhetoric of Laughter,* 107.

instance, is fond of using the mirror to reveal the "horribly grotesque and distorted face" lurking just beneath his "perfectly bland and placid" disguise (*OCS*, 40)—but it is the first in which mirrors are spread so liberally throughout the text. The sense of simultaneous opposition and identification experienced when gazing into a mirror parallels the situation of characters struggling against relatives or countrymen or friends, that is, the situation of most of the characters in the novel. Sim Tappertit, John Chester, Dolly Varden, Emma Haredale, Hugh, Barnaby Rudge, and John Willet are all described, in some cases repeatedly, as examining or resembling reflections in a looking glass, and seven of the novel's original illustrations picture mirrors in six different locations. "Five hundred flickering fires" are "reflected" in the pots and pans and polished furniture of the Maypole Inn (*BR*, 248). In a scene that anticipates the imagistic complexity of *Little Dorrit,* John Chester is confronted by Hugh, his unacknowledged son, as Chester sits before his glass:

> [Hugh's] own rough speech, contrasted with the soft persuasive accents of the other; his rude bearing, and Mr. Chester's polished manner; the disorder and negligence of his ragged dress, and the elegant attire he saw before him; with all the unaccustomed luxuries and comforts of the room, and the silence that gave him leisure to observe these things, and feel how ill at ease they made him . . . , quelled Hugh completely. He moved by little and little nearer to Mr. Chester's chair, . . . glancing over his shoulder at the reflection of his face in the glass, as if seeking some kind of encouragement in its expression. (*BR*, 176)

In one of the novel's most characteristic moments, Hugh is gazing at a man who is on the one hand his physical and social antithesis and on the other his father, his creator; Chester all the while is gazing at his own reflection, that is, at himself reversed. Near the end of the passage, Hugh is also gazing at Chester's reflection—the opposite of his opposite—perhaps suggesting that the chasm between the two is not so wide as it appears to be and that Hugh, in gazing at an image of Chester, is unknowingly gazing at an image of his own begetter. Once again the tensions within and between characters are emphasized and the borders of individual identity blurred.

The most overt double image of Dickens's middle period appears in *The Haunted Man,* the Christmas book of 1848, where the protagonist Redlaw is confronted by a spectral version of himself—not a ghost, precisely, but a phantom projection of his own unhappy past whose reality or unreality is left open to question. Opinions about the

merits of *The Haunted Man* are sharply divided, but virtually all the
(relatively few) critics who comment upon the story acknowledge its
autobiographical implications.[13] Perhaps because it was the latest of
the Christmas books, composed only shortly before *David Copperfield,* it reveals a clear concern with the fragility of internal life and,
as Ruth Glancy suggests, "anticipates [in economy and psychological
complexity] the novels which succeeded it."[14] The manuscript of the
story shows evidence of careful planning and extensive revision;[15]
more important, the story itself, unlike the earlier Christmas stories, shows evidence of Dickens's engagement with the complexities
of character representation. The description of Redlaw with which
The Haunted Man begins recalls the doubtful, polysemous style of
Dickens's mature fiction:

> Who could have seen his hollow cheek, his sunken brilliant eye; his black
> attired figure, indefinably grim, although well-knit and well-proportioned;
> his grizzled hair hanging, like tangled sea-weed about his face,—as if he
> had been, through his whole life, a lonely mark for the chafing and beating
> of the great deep of humanity,—but might have said he looked like a
> haunted man?
>
> Who could have observed his manner, taciturn, thoughtful, gloomy,
> shadowed by habitual reserve, retiring always and jocund never, with a
> distraught air of reverting to a bygone place and time, or of listening to
> some old echoes in his mind, but might have said it was the manner of a
> haunted man?
>
> Who could have heard his voice, slow-speaking, deep, and grave, with
> a natural fulness and melody in it which he seemed to set himself against
> and stop, but might have said it was the voice of a haunted man?
>
> Who that had seen him in his inner chamber. . . . who that had seen him
> then, his work done, and he pondering in his chair before the rusted grate
> and red flame, moving his thin mouth as if in speech, but silent as the dead,
> would not have said that the man seemed haunted and the chamber too?
> (*CB,* 317–18)

13. Alexander Welsh initially pronounces *The Haunted Man* "a poor story
with inconsistencies and a few unintelligible sentences" *(City of Dickens,* 101);
later, however, he seems to view it more favorably, calling it "biographically and
psychologically the most revealing" of the Christmas books and "prototypic of
psychoanalysis." See *From Copyright to Copperfield: The Identity of Dickens,*
101. John Lucas judges the story "inconsiderable" but "inevitably of interest" as
an autobiographical anticipation of *David Copperfield,* in *Melancholy Man,* 168.
Deborah A. Thomas, on the other hand, considers *The Haunted Man* "artistically
controlled" *(Dickens and the Short Story,* 52), and Harry Stone argues that
it surpasses the other Christmas books "in its sophisticated fusion of realism,
psychology, and allegory," in *Invisible World,* 140.
     14. Ruth Glancy, "Dickens at Work on *The Haunted Man,*" 65.
     15. See Glancy, *"Haunted Man,"* 65–86, and Peter Ackroyd, *Dickens,* 553–54.

Few passages in Dickens prior to the 1850s are so strongly marked by the language of doubt. The uncertainty of "could have," "might have," and "would have," the hesitancy of "as if" and "seemed," and the self-qualification of "although" and "but" signal a struggle to perceive and understand Redlaw that is utterly absent from the confident presentation of Scrooge. Whereas the earlier character is little more than the central piece in an extended allegory, the later one is a study of psychological self-division and from the beginning is approached with more circumspection.

Redlaw's confrontation with his double is another example of the "divided mind . . . engaged in a dialogue with itself,"[16] complete with Dickens's characteristic images of mirroring and staring. Like a reflection in a looking glass, Redlaw's "awful likeness" re-creates his movements and expressions: "As *he* leaned his arm upon the elbow of his chair, ruminating before the fire, *it* leaned upon the chair-back, close above him, with its appalling copy of his face looking where his face looked, and bearing the expression his face bore." A moment later "the haunted man turned, suddenly, and stared upon the Ghost. The Ghost, as sudden in its motion, passed to before the chair, and stared on him" (*CB*, 330–31). Most interesting in terms of Dickens's characterization is the bargain offered by the Ghost to Redlaw: forgetfulness of "the sorrow, wrong, and trouble you have known" (*CB*, 334), that is, of unhappy memories, and existence in a pastless, painless present. He offers, in other words, to excise that portion of the consciousness that leads to self-division and self-deception in characters such as Clennam, Flora, Tattycoram, Pet, and many others. Eventually, after an extended trial period, Redlaw declines the "fatal gift" (*CB*, 376), the boldly writ moral being that remembrance and forgiveness are both more Christian and more fulfilling than oblivion. The psychological "moral" appears to be that the tension and energy generated by duality are preferable to the stability of the undivided self. In effect Redlaw opts to be Arthur Clennam rather than Nicholas Nickleby.

While literal twins (as opposed to figurative doubles such as Clennam and Rigaud) recur relatively infrequently in Dickens, mirrors appear at critical moments in nearly all his novels, often suggesting fractured or dual identity. The divisions within Edith Dombey and Esther Summerson, for instance, are given concrete form through reflections in a glass. In yet another image of multiple doubling, Sydney

16. Stone, *Invisible World*, 139.

Carton, after parting from Charles Darnay, considers himself in "a glass hung against the wall": " 'Do you particularly like the man?' he muttered, at his own image; 'why should you particularly like a man who resembles you? . . . Come on, and have it out in plain words! You hate the fellow' " (*TTC*, 79). The external doubling of Carton by Darnay parallels the internal division within Carton himself, a connection reinforced by the deliberate ambiguity of Carton's imprecations: the "fellow" he hates is both Darnay and his own second self as embodied in the reflection. *A Tale of Two Cities* is also, like *Little Dorrit,* a novel in which the shadow image plays a central role and in which explicit linkages are made between the "shadows within" individuals and the "shadows without" that darken the landscape (*TTC*, 336).[17]

Dickens's reliance on the imagery of doubling, like his more general concern with the dissolution of identity, appears to crest in his last two novels, where twinning, mirroring, and similar acts of duplication are regularly foregrounded. *Our Mutual Friend* focuses attention on the fragmentation of personality through the multiple identities of John Harmon and the complex parallels among the three male protagonists. It presents as well several striking images of self-division.[18] When Bradley Headstone, as part of his plot to murder Eugene Wrayburn, dresses in the clothes of Rogue Riderhood, the identities of the two men break apart and interweave, Riderhood addressing Headstone as "myself" and Headstone, internally chaotic to begin with, appearing to lose all sense of a stable self: "whereas, in his own schoolmaster clothes, he usually looked as if they were the clothes of some other man, he now looked, in the clothes of some other man, as if they were his own" (*OMF,* 631). Particularly recurrent, Juliet McMaster has observed, are "images split and refracted, as through a rippled surface or a cracked mirror"[19]—images, that is, very much like those in *Little Dorrit,* where the mirrors seem always defective and where Miss Wade is first glimpsed watching "the reflection of the water as it made a silver quivering on the bars of the lattice" (*LD,* 23). In *Our Mutual Friend,* Georgina Podsnap's picture of the world is "principally derived

---

17. See Sylvère Monod, "Some Stylistic Devices in *A Tale of Two Cities,*" 171–72.

18. J. Hillis Miller in fact argues that here, even more than in *Bleak House,* the structure of the novel "is formed by the juxtaposition of incompatible fragments in a pattern of disharmony or mutual contradiction." See *World,* 284.

19. Juliet McMaster, *Dickens the Designer,* 199.

from the reflections of it in her father's boots, and in the walnut and rosewood table in the dim drawing-room" (*OMF*, 130). The unhappily married Lammles create reflected second selves more honest than the originals: "There was a mirror on the wall before them, and her eyes just caught him smirking in it. She gave the reflected image a look of the deepest disdain, and the image received it in the glass. Next moment they quietly eyed each other, as if they, the principals, had had no part in that expressive transaction" (*OMF*, 260). Here and throughout the novel "there is some emphasis on the reflected image as having its own existence distinct from what it reflects,"[20] as Ephraim Flintwinch exists apart from his brother or Redlaw's specter apart from the original. The mirror divides or multiplies the character into connected yet opposed selves.

The best known and most extensively developed mirror image in Dickens appears in the second chapter of *Our Mutual Friend,* where "the great looking-glass above the sideboard" reflects the guests at the Veneerings' dinner party:

> Reflects Veneering; forty, wavy-haired, dark, tending to corpulence, sly, mysterious, filmy. . . . Reflects Mrs. Veneering; fair, aquiline-nosed and fingered, not so much light hair as she might have. . . . Reflects Podsnap; prosperously feeding, two little light-coloured wiry wings, one on either side of his else bald head. . . . Reflects Mrs. Podsnap; fine woman for Professor Owen, quantity of bone, neck and nostrils like a rocking-horse. . . . Reflects Twemlow; grey, dry, polite, susceptible to east wind. . . . Reflects mature young lady; raven locks, and complexion that lights up when well powdered. (*OMF*, 10)

So the passage pushes on through another twenty or so lines, introducing into the novel a fair number of its major characters. The insistently repetitive sentence structure—subject-ellipsis, "Reflects," character, semicolon, elaborate descriptive phrase—continues unchanged to the end of the long paragraph, freezing the moment in time and underscoring, if not belaboring, the importance of the mirror image. But what is that importance? On one level the reflection carries further the implications of the name "Veneering" and, as Kaplan notes, begins the novel's criticism of "a shiny surface world of superficial people and things"; it serves too as what John Romano calls an "ambivalent and doubtful . . . emblem of the mimetic art of [the] novel," conveying

20. Ibid., 199. Kaplan discusses the same moment in *Mesmerism,* 114, as does Steven Connor in *Charles Dickens,* 147.

Dickens's sense of what his representational medium can and cannot accomplish.[21] As I have attempted to demonstrate, Dickens's doubts about the potential for the novelist to penetrate beneath the surface of reality, even adequately to perceive the surface, lie at the heart of and shape his enterprise, particularly by this late stage in his career. The limitations of the mirror—both its flatness and its confinement within a frame—at least invite comparison to the limitations imposed upon the novelist.

For my purposes, the looking glass is most interesting as a paradigmatic expression of Dickens's uncertainty about the existence of a unified, essential self. The figures reflected there enter the novel through descriptions of their doubles. The relation between the original and the double, moreover, is more ambiguous than it might initially appear to be. On the one hand, the mirror image is a surface reproduction that can never reveal any underlying depth; on the other, as the reflected exchange of the Lammles demonstrates, the mirror seems capable of displaying truths kept hidden in the three-dimensional world. Dickens was doubtless aware that looking glasses were employed to "intensify" the mesmeric force by Elliotson and others, who believed that the mirror "could be used not only to heighten reality but to reveal the actual. One could see in the mirror a reality that was not accessible in the illusions of unreflecting surfaces."[22] Certainly the unremitting harshness of the long description suggests not that the mirror presents shiny, superficial images, but that it probes beneath the surface; or, at the very least, that the surfaces displayed within the mirror are unlike those outside it. The characters and their reflections are no more interchangeable than Carton and Darnay.

The Mystery of Edwin Drood continues the imagery of the imperfect, self-dividing mirror—Mr. Grewgious, for example, addresses his likeness in "the misty looking-glass" as if it is some other "poor man" (*ED*, 126)—and includes, in Neville and Helena Landless, the Dickensian twins most openly representative of the dual personality. To a greater degree even than Minnie and Lillie Meagles, the Landlesses form an indissoluble unit that violates the ordinary boundaries between individuals. " 'You don't know . . .' " Neville tells Mr. Crisparkle, " 'what a complete understanding can exist between my sister and me, though no spoken word—perhaps hardly as much

21. Kaplan, *Mesmerism*, 117; Romano, *Dickens and Reality*, 30.
22. Kaplan, *Mesmerism*, 113.

as a look—may have passed between us. She not only feels as I have described, but she very well knows that I am taking this opportunity of speaking to you, both for her and for myself'" (*ED*, 64). This mesmeric connection is reinforced by the almost neutered identicality of the twins—both "slender, supple, . . . half shy, half defiant"— and by Helena's history of "dress[ing] as a boy, and show[ing] the daring of a man" (*ED*, 56, 63). At the same time, the Landlesses, like the Flintwinches, possess complementary personalities, Neville's indecisiveness and easily manipulated passion being counterbalanced by Helena's "masterful" (*ED*, 67) strength and control. In this novel where "division, split personality, [and] the divided life . . . are basic characterising principles,"[23] the Landlesses form a literal, external example of the two natures that coexist within Miss Twinkleton, Edwin Drood, Mr. Grewgious, and, preeminently, John Jasper.

The best way to understand these various images may be as typically Dickensian eruptions to the surface of concerns underlying the narrative, much like the discussions of uncertain language in texts stylistically uncertain or the more overt examples of split personality in texts populated by internally fragmented characters. Now and then Dickens seems compelled to make the forces and fears that are giving shape to a novel the subject of the novel itself—not for very long and not too explicitly, but long enough and explicitly enough to be noticeable. His creation of character is dominated by his suspicion that personality is neither unified nor stable and that one's attempt to understand the essential nature of any individual, even oneself, is at best an imprecise enterprise. So periodically in his novels a character glimpses a frighteningly unfamiliar figure in a mirror, or confronts an identical but complementary twin, or is trailed by a monstrous shadow, and the uncertainty underlying the apparent stability of the self is momentarily revealed. At such times the reader is in the position of Affery Flintwinch, trying to distinguish between an object and its reflection, the original and its double, "with her head going round and round" (*LD*, 42).

23. James A. Davies, *Textual Life*, 126.

6

"TOTALLY UNCALLED FOR BY
ANYTHING SAID BY ANYBODY"
Character and Structure

O F THE MANY LUNATICS, eccentrics, and idiosyncratic an-
archists in Dickens, possibly the most peculiar, or at least
the most impervious to traditional forms of critical interpretation, is Mr. F's Aunt—an intimidating figure who, according to
Alan Wilde, resists " 'realistic' explication as stolidly as she resists
Clennam's attempts to propitiate her."[1] The actions and remarks of
this solipsist make no sense to the other characters in the story (with
the interesting exception, to be discussed shortly, of Flora Finching),
and she in turn appears neither to see nor to hear them. In the plot
she serves no observable purpose, and to the complex networks of
symbolic and thematic meaning in *Little Dorrit* she bears only the
most tenuous relation. One might put forward the old argument that
Dickens simply cannot construct and is given to such excrescences,
except that the self-enclosure of Mr. F's Aunt is so extreme and so
openly acknowledged: Dickens not only makes no attempt to disguise
her irrelevancy, but regularly draws attention to it. Often his remarks
about her appear to highlight the special exegetical problems she poses
to the would-be critic:

> The major characteristics discoverable by the stranger in Mr. F's Aunt,
> were extreme severity and grim taciturnity; sometimes interrupted by a
> propensity to offer remarks in a deep warning voice, which, being totally
> uncalled for by anything said by anybody, and traceable to no association
> of ideas, confounded and terrified the mind. Mr. F's Aunt may have thrown
> in these observations on some system of her own, and it may have been
> ingenious, or even subtle; but the key to it was wanted. (*LD*, 157)

Who searches more avidly than the critic for an "association of ideas,"
for "some system . . . ingenious, or even subtle," and, above all, for the

---

1. Alan Wilde, "Mr. F's Aunt and the Analogical Structure of *Little Dorrit*," 36.

ultimate interpretive "key"? The "stranger" in this passage is actually anyone who attempts to forge conventional connections between characters and the books they inhabit. As he does regularly in *Little Dorrit*, Dickens is demonstrating here his awareness of the characteristic transactions between text and reader, and particularly of the reader's continual desire to find understandable meaning and definitive form. Once more he foregrounds in a self-reflexive moment a tension—this time between a character's dependence on and independence from a text—that can be felt more subtly throughout the novel.

Mr. F's Aunt has not proven utterly resistant to interpretation (what could?), though by and large critics of *Little Dorrit* have wisely steered clear of her. Wilde makes the most ambitious case for her importance, arguing that she sits at "the heart of the novel" as "the analogical center of the chaotic forces that pervade it": her reification into "a staring wooden doll too cheap for expression" typifies the process of dehumanization in the novel's dark world, and her "extreme severity," "grim taciturnity," and "bitterness" exemplify its tone (*LD*, 157–58).[2] He considers her, in effect, a Mrs. Clennam robbed of clear motivation or the ability to communicate. More recently, and more convincingly, both Elaine Showalter and Natalie McKnight have suggested that Mr. F's Aunt acts, in Showalter's words, as "the embodiment of Flora's repressed anger at Arthur's rejection," in much the same way that Maggy acts out the repressed appetites of Little Dorrit: "Flora," McKnight writes, " . . . needs Mr. F's Aunt as an alter ego, for the old lady uses her proclamations to vent some spleen, something Flora never does or never is able to do."[3] This makes good sense. Nevertheless, it seems to me that the dominant effect of Mr. F's Aunt on the reader, and the effect to which the narrative most insistently draws attention, is to disorient, disturb, confuse. Each of her ominous non sequiturs—an offer of port is followed by the proclamation that " 'The monument near London Bridge . . . was put up arter the Great Fire of London; and the Great Fire of London was not the fire in which your uncle George's workshops was burned down' " (*LD*, 159)—acts as a reminder not only of her disconnection from reality but also of her character's

---

2. Ibid., 37. About thirty years ago Wilde noted that "the only critic who makes (slightly) more than passing reference to Mr. F's Aunt is Jack Lindsay in his *Charles Dickens* (London, 1950)," 34. Since then critics have remained comparably mum, with the important exceptions of those noted in this chapter.

3. Showalter, "Guilt," 37; McKnight, *Idiots, Madmen,* 123.

disconnection from the narrative, thematic, and symbolic structures that surround it. "The effect of [her] mysterious communication[s] upon Clennam was absolutely to frighten him" (*LD*, 158); the reader might well be frightened, a little, by her violation of the ordinary expectation that characters exist because of, not independent of or even in spite of, the novels within which they are contained. Mr. F's Aunt's brief, infrequent appearances read like the periodic irruptions of a second, alien text into the fabric of *Little Dorrit*.

If Mr. F's Aunt is a nearly opaque text, then Flora Finching establishes the initial claim as her explicator. Alone among the characters in *Little Dorrit*, Flora receives each remark of Mr. F's Aunt "as if it had been of a most apposite and agreeable nature" and "without the least discomposure or surprise" (*LD*, 269, 537). Repeatedly she endeavors to translate her companion's irrelevant outbursts into terms that make contextual sense—to fit her, that is, into the plot and structure of the novel. Her attempts, however, are at best mild parodies of, and at worst dismissive attacks on, the interpretive activities of the critic: they seem wholly unable to penetrate the mystery of the old woman and reveal more about the priorities of the interpreter than about the purported object of interpretation. Mr. F's Aunt means no more and no less than Flora wants her to mean. That all subsequent interpreters of Mr. F's Aunt are destined to follow in Flora's footsteps is suggested by the narrator's final comments on "this admirably consistent female": all suppositions regarding her meaning are of necessity "mere speculation," and her intentions "will never be positively known" (*LD*, 821). One is reminded here of another failed critic, the narrator of Melville's "Bartleby, the Scrivener," who confesses at the end of his exegesis that "upon what basis it rested, I could never ascertain; and hence, how true it is I cannot now tell."[4] Mr. F's Aunt, like Bartleby, is finally *about* the limits of interpretation, both human and textual.

Probably the most fundamental division in recent character criticism is between those who believe character to be wholly defined by the needs of a particular literary structure, or even to be indistinguishable from other portions of that structure, and those who believe it to possess a larger, more autonomous life that transcends structural needs and sets it apart from other structural elements. Already a number

4. Herman Melville, "Bartleby, the Scrivener: A Story of Wall Street," 45.

of scholars have surveyed at length the history of the structuralist approach to character, which may be represented generally by Steven Connor's assessment that "characters are the symptoms of structure, or at best a kind of allegory of structure."[5] According to this view, it is a mistake to differentiate between character and other recurrent items in a text—"a passion, a memory, the weather, Gogol's overcoat . . . a stone in a stream or that soap in Bloom's pocket"[6]—since all are given meaning entirely by the plot and have no significance or existence outside of textual language. Characters are no more like actual people than are the letters "A" and "B" and should not provoke the responses people do.

In the determinedly extreme positions of structuralists and semioticians such as Vladimir Propp, Tzvetan Todorov, and Roland Barthes,[7] character dissolves entirely into the text, even into the structure of language itself, and ceases to exist as an analyzable concept; and, maybe more controversially, the commonly held belief that readers respond to characters as if they were representations of people is dismissed as a myth fostered by humanistic criticism. Todorov "proposes . . . to treat characters as proper names to which certain qualities are attached during the course of the narrative. Characters are not heroes, villains, or helpers; they are simply subjects of a group of predicates which the reader adds up as he goes along." Barthes treats the character not as a being with "a future, an unconscious, a soul," but as "a (transitory) site" where features intersect and that "allows the substitution of a nominal unit for a collection of characteristics."[8] Within the context of such criticism the mention of personality seems no more apposite, perhaps less apposite, than the mention of the workings of an automobile transmission.

Out of these extreme positions have emerged structuralist approaches less linguistically oriented and more willing to acknowledge an emphasis on character as "a fact of reading" rather than a mere "ideological prejudice."[9] Jonathan Culler, for one, distinguishes between the most typical and pleasurable responses to literature and

5. Connor, *Charles Dickens*, 28. See Culler, *Structuralist Poetics*, 230–38; Hochman, *Character*, 13–27; and Phelan, *Reading People*, 3–10.

6. Gass, *Fiction*, 50.

7. "It would not be wrong to suggest that structuralism and semiology are identical." Culler, *Structuralist Poetics*, 6.

8. Ibid., 235; Roland Barthes, *S/Z: An Essay*, 94–95.

9. Culler, *Structuralist Poetics*, 230.

the stance most usefully assumed by the critic. "The most intense and satisfying reading experiences," he writes, "may depend upon what we call involvement with characters, but successful critical investigation of the structure and effects of a novel, as a literary construct, may require thinking of characters as sets of predicates grouped under proper names."[10] Engagement with characters as representations of people, in other words, is no more relevant to a structuralist appraisal than is engagement with characters in a television soap opera to someone trying to adjust the quality of the picture on the screen. Such engagement may, in fact, make it more difficult to adjust the picture by drawing attention away from the characters as patterns of light and color. Others including Connor, Thomas Docherty, and Robert Higbie have retained "character" as a workable concept while attacking the tendency of mimetic theory to make "the character the focus of interest in an unproblematical way" or to "single out one factor of narrative language, the tendency to congeal into named characters, and pin upon this feature all our hopes of elucidating the structure." The shared position of these critics, who recurrently refer to mimetic approaches as naive, is summarized by Joel Weinsheimer: "Once it is admitted that characters are not persons, they are absorbed into text. Closure neutralizes the differentiation of characters from each other and from text."[11]

The "naive" version of mimetic theory most often attacked in structuralist work is not at present a major feature of character criticism and has not been for some time. To return to the quotations above, few theorists recently have made characters the focus of interest in an "unproblematical way" or have pinned upon characters "all" hopes of elucidating structure.[12] Rather, antistructuralist or mimetic critics tend to grant the dependence of character on structure but to deny that such dependence is absolute or that characters are indistinguishable

---

10. Jonathan Culler, "Issues in Contemporary American Critical Debate," 5.

11. Docherty, *(Absent) Character*, xii; Connor, *Charles Dickens*, 27–28; Joel Weinsheimer, "Theory of Character: *Emma*," 208. See also Higbie, *Character and Structure*.

12. To be fair, mimetic critics have often been as extreme in their characterizations of the structuralist position. Baruch Hochman's claim that "On the whole, the structuralists have held that character does not emerge as a detachable or independent element in our consciousness during or after reading" is true only of the most purely structuralist criticism and does not represent, for instance, the position of Culler. See Hochman, *Character*, 27.

from other recurrent linguistic elements. Because characters are representations of people, they have the power to provoke the kind of speculation and inference that the letter "A" or even the soap in Bloom's pocket does not and to generate meaning inexplicable on a structural level. From this perspective, to understand character in purely structural terms is not merely to read incompletely but, potentially, to read incorrectly: "Where the structuralist remains suspicious of the emotional involvement that comes from viewing the character as a possible person," James Phelan writes, "the mimetic analyst regards that involvement as crucial to the effect of the work." The operative word in such criticism appears to be "autonomy," as when Seymour Chatman argues that "a viable theory of character should preserve openness and treat characters as autonomous beings, not as mere plot functions," or Martin Price that "a character, for all the conventions of his literary life, may acquire some degree of autonomy." Autonomy in this context does not mean, of course, that a character may stride off the page into physical life as in some fantasy of Pirandello, but that it may possess meaning, provoke responses, or invite speculation that has little to do with the plot, themes, or even language of the text within which it exists. "Character," insists Baruch Hochman, "is . . . separable from the text, along lines dictated by the text."[13]

To some extent at least the disagreement between structuralist and mimetic critics is a disagreement over the definition of terms: one's argument rests on what one means by such elusive words as "character" and "text." The apprehension of characterization, indeed of all representational art, is a collaborative process in the sense described by many reader-response critics or, even earlier, by E. H. Gombrich in his discussion of the perceptual response to painting. "The painter," Gombrich writes, "relies on our readiness to take hints, to read contexts, and to call up our conceptual image under his guidance. The blob in the painting by Manet which stands for a horse is no more an imitation of its external form than is [a] hobby horse. But he has so cleverly contrived it that it evokes the image in us—provided, of course, we collaborate."[14] Where in fact does Manet's

    13. Phelan, *Reading People*, 8; Chatman, *Story and Discourse*, 119; Price, *Forms of Life*, 58; Hochman, *Character*, 32.
    14. E. H. Gombrich, *Meditations on a Hobby Horse and Other Essays on the Theory of Art*, 10. "What is relevant, and how do we know?" Susan R. Horton has written more recently. "What constitutes a 'part': the word? the sentence? the

horse end and the viewer's begin? To argue that Manet has provided no more than an irregular blob of paint is to ignore the undeniable fact that this blob, as opposed to thousands of others in the painting, has in its context the power to suggest "horse"; to argue that he has provided a reproduction of a horse is to ignore the many details left out. Similarly, to argue as William Gass does that "characters in fiction are mostly empty canvas" raises the question of whether the details automatically "filled in" by the reader should be considered part of or apart from the character itself—intratextual or extratextual?[15] When Ebenezer Scrooge laments in *A Christmas Carol* that he "should like to be able to say a word or two to my clerk just now" (*CB*, 33), is the speculation about what those words might be—clearly invited and directed by the story—part of or apart from the text? Where does the entity designated by the word "character" stop and the reader's response to that character begin? On these questions there is nothing approaching universal agreement—though Wolfgang Iser's definition of an "implied reader" who "produces a meaning which is neither wholly determinate . . . nor entirely subjective" strikes a useful compromise.[16]

My intention here is not to propose a resolution of the argument between structuralists and what one might call "autonomists," or even to champion a particular camp (though my bias against a purely structuralist reading of character is inscribed implicitly and explicitly throughout this study). Rather it is to suggest, first, that the tension between the structural dependence of characters and the reader's inclination to imagine independence is inherently a part of the reading (and interpreting) process; and second, that Dickens seems aware of and deliberately tries to intensify that tension in his fiction—to both invite and frustrate the search for structural relevance. That he at least sends mixed signals on this issue of structural dependence versus autonomy is indicated by the frequency with which both structuralist and mimetic critics draw upon his novels for supporting evidence. The intricacy of his fictional constructs and the subtlety of the relations among his characters, symbols, and themes yield nicely to structuralist analysis;

---

mode of presentation? the chapter? What is a 'text,' and what are its boundaries: all of the writer's words? all language?" *Interpreting Interpreting: Interpreting Dickens's Dombey*, 5.

15. Gass is quoted from *Fiction*, 45.

16. Summarized by Catherine Belsey in *Critical Practice*, 35–36.

again and again, careful attention to underlying structure shows the apparently irrelevant to be relevant, the apparently meaningless to be meaningful. The "failure" of Dickens's fiction by the traditional standards of mimetic criticism, moreover, has invited other approaches that might better account for its success. So the structuralist critic Michael Squires can, by exposing a network of recurrent patterns, tie an apparently superfluous character such as Flintwinch to the most important ideas and images in *Little Dorrit* and rescue the novel from charges of disorganization.[17]

At the same time, Dickens's characters are distinguished by their tendency to transcend or resist the requirements, or what Price calls the "demands," of structure, as the extreme but representative example of Mr. F's Aunt demonstrates. Similarly, the sheer excessiveness with which Flintwinch terrorizes his wife, torments his employer, and plots against Clennam plays no clear structural role and may in fact work against structure by implying the existence of motives and plots that never materialize. Dickens's characters, according to Robert Higbie, "often act in an excessive manner; [his] characterization is full of superlatives and descriptions of extremeness" that are never convincingly explained.[18] The later novels especially invite the discovery or construction of an elaborate organizing structure while destabilizing that structure through characters whose behavior and actions do not appear to belong.

No portion of this book, I suspect, is likely to be met with more disagreement than this discussion of the relations between character and structure. At the risk of belaboring the obvious, therefore, let me try to draw some distinctions more precisely. Narrative structure, of course, need not be "about unilinear, ordered, composed sorts of signification" and may expand to include all varieties of competing, inconsistent, and ambiguous meanings. Characters too need not be imagined as "stable element[s] in a text, about which readers can arrive at consensus."[19] Novels may, indeed the most interesting ones generally do, incorporate challenges to their own overt themes and

---

17. Squires, "Dickens's Imagination," 50–54.

18. Martin Price, "The Logic of Intensity: More on Character," 373; Higbie, *Character and Structure*, 137.

19. I cite here John Kucich's challenges to an earlier version of this argument in "Recent Dickens Studies: 1989," 326. About that earlier version Kucich now seems to me quite right, and I am indebted to his critique in constructing the present chapter.

arguments, and the characters of many novelists aside from Dickens fail sometimes to cohere into discrete personalities or embodiments of value. To claim that a character means A, that a narrative means B, and that the resultant conflict creates a challenge to structure is to treat the concepts of character, narrative, and structure reductively.

In *The Old Curiosity Shop,* for instance, the values and moral precepts espoused by the narrator are called into question by the ambivalent character of Little Nell in a way that complicates the novel but presents no challenge to "structure." On the surface the ethical system of the novel is not complex, and Little Nell seems the character who fits most easily into its broad symbolic categories. Her attributes are those of youth, innocence, goodness, and beauty; her natural realm, the unviolated countryside; her natural desire, to serve. Underscoring Nell's qualities are those of her symbolic and literal antagonist, Daniel Quilp, a grotesque embodiment of ugliness, covetousness, and the threatening energy of the city, whose desire to possess and destroy Nell is evil's desire to possess and destroy its opposite. The novel enacts their conflict and at the end seems to allow no mistake about the "meaning" of its result:

> Oh! it is hard to take to heart the lesson that such deaths will teach, but let no man reject it, for it is one that all must learn, and is a mighty, universal Truth. When Death strikes down the innocent and young, for every fragile form from which he lets the panting spirit free, a hundred virtues rise, in shapes of mercy, charity, and love, to walk the world, and bless it. . . . In the Destroyer's steps spring up bright creations that defy his power, and his dark path becomes a way of light to Heaven. (*OCS,* 544)

The problem with this "lesson" is that it casts Nell as a representative of living benevolence. The narrator's defiance of a Death that "strikes down the innocent and the young" suggests an active, stalking malevolent force that overcomes a helpless character like Nell against her will. Yet as many readers have noticed, Nell not only fails to resist death with much enthusiasm, but seems continually to seek it out and to radiate what Steven Marcus calls a "spiritual necrophilia."[20] Her pastoral yearnings are not toward the cyclical life of the forest but toward the stasis and tranquility of the grave:

> It was yet early, and the old man being still asleep, she walked out into the churchyard, brushing the dew from the long grass with her feet, and

20. Marcus, *Pickwick,* 146.

often turning aside into places where it grew longer than in others, that she might not tread upon the graves. She felt a curious kind of pleasure in lingering among these houses of the dead, and read the inscriptions on the tombs of the good people (a great number of good people were buried there), passing on from one to another with increasing interest. (*OCS*, 128)

Death, contrary to the lamentations of the narrator, can legitimately be seen as helpless against the onslaughts of Nell: try as it might, it cannot escape her. Once one recognizes the death wish implicit in Nell's behavior, the categories of the plot are effectively reversed, and Quilp, the embodiment and agent of Death, becomes from a new perspective a symbol of an irrepressible if dangerous vitality. By working against context, character here complicates one's reading of the novel as a whole, problematizing the plot and challenging the reliability of the narrative voice—but it does not (and this is the crucial point) disrupt "structure," which is broad and flexible enough to incorporate such internal tensions.

Mr. F's Aunt elicits a more unsettling response. Representational art inevitably generates a tension between awareness and transcendence of structure, or between resistance to and participation in the representational illusion. As long as one remains conscious of the presence of language or paint or marble, the illusion cannot fully take hold; as long as one remains caught in the illusion, structural analysis cannot proceed—hence Culler's distinction between "the most intense and satisfying reading experiences" and "successful critical investigation of the structure and effects of a novel."[21] Both things cannot happen at once. The gulf between these two kinds of response may be especially great in realistic fiction, where the difference between structure and illusion—between the language on the page and the world it attempts to create—is so dramatic. While structuralist criticism has tended simply to define "the most intense and satisfying reading experiences" as lying outside the realm of "successful critical investigation," it seems to me that the connections and differences between typical reading experiences on the one hand, and the critical analysis of structure on the other, are themselves a fruitful area of investigation—that, in fact, one of the more distinctive pleasures of reading fiction arises from the interplay between what might be called mimetic and structuralist responses.

21. Culler, "Issues," 5.

Dickens's trick is to include characters and forms of behavior that highlight both the artificiality of the fictional illusion and the inability of structure fully to contain that illusion. Because Mr. F's Aunt invites yet resists "realistic explication" and seems almost ostentatiously disconnected from the represented world of *Little Dorrit*,[22] she reminds the reader of its fictionality—the way a single misplaced piece in a large jigsaw puzzle might rupture the illusion created by the other 499, or the way a fly crawling across the canvas of a landscape painting might dissolve the "reality" of the landscape. That same disconnection, however, seems also to exemplify Hochman's claim that characters are "utterly embedded in texts and absolutely detachable from them," or Chatman's that "some characters in sophisticated narratives remain open constructs, just as some people in the real world stay mysteries no matter how well we know them,"[23] and thus to frustrate a purely structural analysis. She makes complete sense in neither the represented world nor the structure of *Little Dorrit*, except as testimony to the limits of both. Put another way, she invites both the "mimetic" and the "structuralist" reader to recognize the incompleteness of their responses.

Both traditional mimetic and recent structuralist criticism tend, for different reasons, to minimize or overlook the peculiarly disruptive impact of a Mr. F's Aunt. In traditional terms—"A novel is a living organism, all one and continuous, like any other organism, and in proportion as it lives will it be found . . . that in each of the parts there is something of each of the other parts"—she may be dismissed as a vestigial organ, as a figure who never establishes the requisite connections to the trajectory of the narrative. In structuralist terms— "it is not always easy to assign characters to their particular places in the structure, and this is because the structure works through them, rather than vice versa"[24]—her challenge to structure cannot logically exist, any more than the existence of an object can pose a challenge to the integrity of the universe. Both entities, structure and universe, are defined as all-encompassing and not subject to transcendence. Neither approach is of more than limited help in distinguishing between the effects on the reader of Mr. F's Aunt and the effects of other, more easily assimilated characters: from one perspective the absence of

22. Wilde, "Mr. F's Aunt," 36.
23. Hochman, *Character*, 74; Chatman, *Story and Discourse*, 118.
24. James, *Theory of Fiction*, 36; Connor, *Charles Dickens*, 27.

a "key" to her meaning is damning, from the other it is largely irrelevant.

Dickens uses character in at least three typical and interrelated ways to foreground the tension between structural dependence and autonomy. He creates a veritable tribe of characters whose actions and remarks seem, like those of Mr. F's Aunt, "totally uncalled for by anything said by anybody, and traceable to no association of ideas" (*LD,* 157); he presents extreme forms of behavior and response that also seem uncalled for and untraceable, and that suggest the existence of motives or structures that are never otherwise developed or explained; and he includes in many of his novels mysterious characters whose place in the fiction is only defined after an extended period of ambiguity and who seem, even then, persistently disturbing or elusive. These practices, sometimes operating in concert, tend generally to make the attempt to reconcile character and structure an unusually prominent part of the reading process.

The situation of Mr. F's Aunt is anticipated repeatedly in Dickens's earlier fiction, perhaps initially by *Nicholas Nickleby*'s gentleman in small-clothes, another rich source of inappropriate actions and incomprehensible remarks: " 'Tears!' cried the old gentleman, with such an energetic jump, that he fell down two or three steps, and grated his chin against the wall. 'Catch the crystal globules—catch 'em—bottle 'em up—cork 'em tight—put sealing-wax on the top—seal 'em with a cupid—label 'em 'Best quality'—and stow 'em away in the fourteen binn, with a bar of iron on the top to keep the thunder off!' " (*NN,* 536). Though the gentleman in small-clothes seems "mad" in a more conventional and less disturbing sense than Mr. F's Aunt, he manages still to disrupt the apparent transparency and order of the narrative and to gesture toward the instability of personality. In a novel marked by an almost suffocating sense of closure, with explanations provided for all mysteries and appropriate rewards and punishments meted out with formulaic precision, the absence of a definite meaning or role for the gentleman in small-clothes is noteworthy.[25] Like many Dickensian lunatics, he demonstrates the ease with which language can become detached from any clear referent. And he too is given, in Mrs. Nickleby, an obviously unsatisfactory translator determined to

25. Natalie McKnight calls the gentleman in small-clothes "a kind of temporary antidote to the Nicklebys' stuffiness," but one who is, in the interest of restoring order, "eventually excised from the text." See *Idiots, Madmen,* 75–76.

prove that his behavior "was the most rational and reasonable in the world" and exactly that which "discreet and thinking persons might have foreseen" (*NN*, 528–29).

In subsequent novels come similar figures including Barnaby Rudge, Old Chuffey, Jack Bunsby, Mr. Dick, Guster, Miss Flite, Mrs. Small-weed, and the Aged P., along with such confident yet unconvincing translators or interpreters as Captain Cuttle, Betsey Trotwood, and Wemmick. In a recurrent pattern, startling and inconsistent behavior and incomprehensible or semicomprehensible language provoke confusion and disquiet among most other characters and, often, a dubious claim to understanding by one. *Dombey and Son*'s Bunsby "seemed by the expression of his visage always on the look-out for something in the distance, and to have no ocular knowledge of anything within ten miles," and he responds to questions with questions more enigmatic (" 'Whereby . . . why not? If so, what odds? Can any man say otherwise? No. Awast then!' " [*DS*, 335, 338]); Captain Cuttle in turn explains "that Bunsby meant nothing but confidence; that Bunsby had no misgivings; and that such an opinion as that man had given, coming from such a mind as his, was Hope's own anchor, with good roads to cast it in" (*DS*, 339). Again one is reminded that Dickens's linguistic art is founded upon uncertainty about the efficacy of language, and that his character-dominated fiction is marked by worry over the indeterminacy of character. If, as Catherine Belsey argues, classic realism assumes that character is "unified and coherent" and, more fundamentally, that language provides direct access to knowledge of some verifiable reality,[26] then Bunsby and the others provide a challenge to traditional assumptions.

Naturally enough, the sheer lunacy of a Mr. F's Aunt or gentleman in small-clothes can appear only infrequently in a novel and provide only occasional if powerful challenges to the relationship between character and structure. More common are moments in which otherwise rational and explicable characters, whose personalities are defined and motives provided within the plot, behave in inexplicable ways: by carrying expected reactions to utterly unexpected extremes, or by acting on the basis of apparent motives that make no sense within the logic of the narrative. This tendency toward superfluity or gratuitousness has often been identified as one of the signatures of Dickensian characterization,

26. Belsey, *Critical Practice*, 73.

typically as a prelude to criticizing its lack of "realism," but more recently as a means of uncovering and rejecting "realistic" assumptions. Philip Weinstein refers to the "parade of false motives and mixed signals" among Dickens's characters, Robert Higbie to the prevalence of "superlatives and descriptions of extremeness," John Kucich to the tendency of Dickens's villains especially to "act recklessly, gratuitously"; all do so in the context of presenting alternatives to the realistic model of character. What Weinstein calls Dickens's "extravagance" generates characters more self-divided, less stable and discrete, than one ordinarily finds in the nineteenth-century novel.[27] These characters may not transcend "structure" in the broadest sense—that is, the actual language of the text—but they certainly exist in tension with such traditional structural elements as plot, theme, and narrative point of view.

Quilp, who surely acts as gratuitously, recklessly, and extravagantly as any figure in Dickens, dramatizes this tension between character and other elements of structure. His anarchic energy seems directed not just at the other characters, but at the narrative within which he continually refuses to be contained; the "great, goggle-eyed, blunt-nosed figure-head" against which he pounds out his fury—called variously a "portrait," a "representation," and a "substantial phantom"—seems a stand-in not merely for Kit Nubbles, but for the novel itself: " 'Is it like Kit—is it his picture, his image, his very self?' cried the dwarf, aiming a shower of blows at the insensible countenance, and covering it with deep dimples. 'Is it the exact model and counterpart of the dog—is it—is it?' And with every repetition of the question, he battered the great image until the perspiration streamed down his face with the violence of the exercise" (*OCS*, 461). No role defined for Quilp by narrator or plot, theme or symbolic pattern, fully accommodates the extremity and unpredictability of his actions. Whereas Little Nell poses a challenge to the position of the narrator that is in the end fairly coherent, Quilp's challenge is more imposing because more incessant and unpredictable—not a frontal assault but an ongoing series of guerrilla attacks from surprising positions. Though her character may violate the role assigned to it by the narrator or plot, it finally is not, like his, mysterious and elusive. The most convincing attempts to define or delimit Quilp have characterized him as an embodiment of eros

27. Weinstein, *Semantics*, 60; Higbie, *Character and Structure*, 137; Kucich, *Repression*, 210.

or sexuality or desire,[28] but even this understanding does not contain him: he is desire for autonomy let loose within a narrative form that makes autonomy impossible.

One tends to become more conscious of any action, more aware of its peculiarities and parts, as it becomes more arduous to perform. My argument here is that Dickens makes the reader unusually conscious of the desire to understand character in terms of structure by making that understanding difficult to achieve. In another recurrent pattern, he is given to introducing mysterious watchers and followers, shadowy doubles, nameless avengers and protectors, whose motives and identities are kept hidden for an extended period and revealed, finally, through an explanation that seems rational but wholly inadequate. The revelation that Flintwinch's double is merely his drunken brother never fully dissipates the disturbing resonance of their initial, dreamlike encounter or explains Flintwinch's violent pantomime. Monks, a "dark figure" who ordinarily hides in "deep shadow" and moves largely "unperceived" (OT, 191), is Dickens's prototype for such characters, gliding through much of Oliver Twist without a full name, comprehensible motives, or even a clearly discernible form. In subsequent novels his role is reenacted by Mr. Brooker and Mr. Nadgett, Mr. Morfin and Mr. Tulkinghorn, Inspector Bucket and Dick Datchery. Many of these figures are initially mistaken for ghosts or spirits, as Solomon Daisy mistakes the elder Barnaby Rudge, or are perceived, like Ephraim Flintwinch or Nicholas Nickleby's Mr. Brooker, as fragments of a dream:

> "Good Heaven, what is this!" cried Nicholas, bending over him. "Be calm; you have been dreaming."
> "No, no, no!" cried Smike, clinging to him. "Hold me tight. Don't let me go. There—there—behind the tree!"
> Nicholas followed his eyes, which were directed to some distance behind the chair from which he himself had just risen. But there was nothing there.
> "This is nothing but your fancy," he said, as he strove to compose him, "nothing else indeed." (NN, 760–61)

As with objects in a dream, the relation of such characters to context cannot always be rationally understood. "Dickens commonly explains away his mysteries . . . within the novels themselves," notes Albert Guerard. "Thus the character who functions so powerfully

28. See, for instance, Marcus, Pickwick, 152–59; McKnight, Idiots, Madmen, 74; and Chase, Eros and Psyche, 41.

in a dynamic or symbolic role may turn out to be, to our sharp disappointment, a rationally motivated and interested party, say a lost relative or a policeman." But, as Guerard recognizes, the explicable and inexplicable meanings of such characters "do not simply cancel out,"[29] and even after the narrator reveals that Monks is merely a resentful half brother or Bucket a dogged detective, the element of mystery persists. In fact such revelations, granted a privileged status because of the "omniscience" of the narrator, seem only marginally more satisfying than the explanatory efforts of Flora Finching or Captain Cuttle; and as my analysis of Dickens's descriptive language attempted to demonstrate, the narrator's claims to absolute knowledge of character are at best tentative.[30]

Monks, Bucket, and the others carry to an extreme the mystery of personality at the heart of Dickens's fiction. The process through which they are presented—extended uncertainty followed by insufficient explanation—is an exaggerated instance of the process through which the reader apprehends many of Dickens's most interesting characters. Here the mystery is simply more overt, the explanation more obviously unsatisfying; but the sense of personality lying beyond the limits of language and understanding is precisely the one I have been identifying as central to Dickens's characterization. This may be the most basic way in which his characters resist being absorbed into structure, or becoming no more than "symptoms of structure": by refusing to be understood. The definition of characters as "subjects of groups of predicates which the reader adds up as he goes along," as "sets of predicates grouped under proper names," or as "nominal unit[s]" substituting for "a collection of characteristics" implies a process of addition or collection considerably less problematic than the one forced upon the reader who encounters Mr. F's Aunt.[31] The implications of mathematical language such as "adds up" and "sets" are telling: numbers added into a sum or gathered into a set generate a change in size or extent but not in *kind*. A more accurate analogue

29. Albert Guerard, "The Illuminating Distortion," 112, 114.

30. For an extended discussion of the uncertainty inherent in Dickens's omniscient voices, see Audrey Jaffe, *Vanishing Points: Dickens, Narrative, and the Subject of Omniscience.* "Omniscience," Jaffe writes, "is not so much evidence for the possession of knowledge as an emphatic display of knowledge, a display, precisely, of what is not being taken for granted" (6).

31. Connor, *Charles Dickens,* 28; Culler, *Structuralist Poetics,* 235; Culler, "Issues," 5; Barthes, *S/Z,* 94–95.

for the process of characterization might be what takes place in a chemical reaction, where the combination of individual elements or compounds may trigger a dramatic transformation in kind. Because a character such as Mr. F's Aunt is more than the sum of its parts—its associated predicates and accumulated characteristics—it cannot be defined entirely in terms of those parts. The individual actions and statements that compose Mr. F's Aunt are more fully understood, and more comfortably accommodated by structure, than is the "admirably consistent" (*LD*, 821) composite they produce.

Conclusion

The Inimitable

Audrey Jaffe writes, "The assertion of knowledge and authority . . . does not necessarily reflect their secure possession."[1] In fact, she suggests, the most emphatic assertions often signal the presence of the most profound uncertainties and insecurities, so that, for instance, the dominance of omniscient narrative in the nineteenth century may reflect a loss of faith in the possibility of absolute knowledge. The example of Dickens lends this argument force. Few novelists make more powerful claims, inside or outside their fiction, to knowledge of "reality" generally and character specifically, yet few manifest more extreme uncertainty about the reliability of such knowledge; few combine such command of language with such doubt about the efficacy of language. The Inimitable, the (self-coined) epithet of which Dickens was so fond, might be used as well to define the human personality as it seems imagined in his fiction: like Dickens himself, it lies beyond precise imitation or representation—even by one with Dickens's "inimitable" abilities. His faith in those abilities may only have encouraged him to understand his struggles to depict character as inevitable and universal.

Nineteenth-century realistic fiction is frequently imagined, even today, as a confident attempt to represent assumed truths, especially by theorists seeking to demonstrate the fragility of that confidence and the ephemeral nature of those truths. Too often it is constructed as blind to its own characteristic evasions and contradictions. So Catherine Belsey can describe "classic realist texts" in which "the reader is invited to perceive and judge the 'truth' of the text, the coherent, non-contradictory interpretation of the world as it is perceived by an author whose autonomy is the source and evidence of the truth of the interpretation." Classic realism

> tends to offer as the "obvious" basis of its intelligibility the assumption that character, unified and coherent, is the source of action. . . .

1. Jaffe, *Vanishing Points*, 5.

> [It] cannot foreground contradiction. The logic of its structure—the
> movement towards closure—precludes the possibility of leaving the reader
> simply to confront the contradictions which the text may have defined. . . .
> When contradiction exists in classic realism it does so in the margins of
> [the] text.[2]

Belsey is right in noting that the logic of realist fiction seems to work
against openness, incoherence, and contradiction. What she underes-
timates is the extent to which the working out of that logic is a deliberate, if disguised, act of desperation, a consequence not of confidence in
coherence but of desire for coherence. The elaborateness and intensity
of many nineteenth-century attempts at realistic representation reflect
uncertainty about whether such attempts can succeed, and thus there *is*
no realism, at least of an interesting kind, without doubt. To consign
contradiction to the "margins" of the nineteenth-century text is to
define the margins as occupying most of the frame.

Marshall Brown seems to me to capture the nature of nineteenth-
century fiction more accurately when he writes that "realism developed into a central issue in mid-century precisely because the
conception of reality had become increasingly problematic. . . . The
realistic novel can be considered an exploratory investigation into
the nature of reality. The complexity of realism as a mode or as an
effect can then be seen to result from the tentativeness and difficulty
of the search for reality"—and, I would add, of the search for a means
to represent it. Brown identifies Dickens as one of several "haunted
and . . . characteristically realistic writers" of midcentury, characteristic precisely because he *is* haunted rather than untroubled by the
elusiveness of "truth." This is probably why Dickens has occupied so
variable a position in discussions and definitions of realism, sometimes
being placed outside the "realistic" tradition as a writer of romance
or of something more idiosyncratic, sometimes being held up as an
exemplar of the tradition. In the rather automatic, unself-conscious
tradition described by Belsey, Dickens seems out of place; in the more
self-divided tradition described by Brown, "Dickens' epistomological
skepticism . . . is exemplary."[3]

2. Belsey, *Critical Practice*, 68–69, 73, 82.
3. Marshall Brown, "The Logic of Realism: A Hegelian Approach," 227–28,
239*n15*. "Perhaps," Brown writes, "this is why so much recent discussion of
realism in England has concerned Dickens even though he was hostile to the
term" (239*n15*).

That epistomological skepticism works in a number of related ways to produce the effects described in this study. At the heart of Dickens's characterization is doubt about the unity and coherence of personality as profound as, if more troubled than, anything found in postmodern psychological theory—a stance, according to Karen Chase, "as much post- as pre-Jamesian." In the presentation of what Chase calls "personality in a Pickwickian sense," the "integrity of a single point of view breaks down."[4] Character becomes fragmented, self-contradictory, divided within and among individuals. It takes little probing to see that the kind of "closure" that "precludes the possibility of leaving the reader simply to confront the contradictions which the text may have defined" is, at best, sporadically achieved: the contradictory sides of Tattycoram are never reconciled, the multiple roles played by Clennam or Little Dorrit are never fused into a stable whole, the traits spread among the members of the Casby household are never gathered within a single individual. The nature of personality is not a given but a problem.

Dickens is equally skeptical of the bases on which one ordinarily makes guesses about the personalities of others. Speech, appearance, and behavior are susceptible to misreading by even the most perspicacious observer and to deceptive manipulation, malicious or not, by the subject under observation. Even if individual details can be observed clearly and accurately, there is no guarantee that they will yield reliable meaning or that the meaning of particulars will coalesce into the meaning of a larger whole: as George Eliot writes in *Daniel Deronda*, when it comes to observing others "we recognize the alphabet; we are not sure of the language." Again, in one of the ironies of realism, a "collapse of faith in the dominant reality of the empirically verifiable" is accompanied by brilliant, sustained acts of empirical observation, not because the value of such acts is taken for granted but because it is questioned. Doubts about the reliability of observation create a situation in which no amount of observation is ever enough, no volume of detail ever creates a secure base of knowledge.[5]

Maybe most troubling to Dickens is the suspicion that, to paraphrase Rigaud/Lagnier/Blandois, words are without the kinds of power upon which the novelist depends: the power to identify a precise

4. Chase, *Eros and Psyche*, 38, 29.
5. The first quotation in this paragraph is from Eliot, *Daniel Deronda*, 98; the second is from Levine, "Realism Reconsidered," 252.

referent, to convey a clear meaning, to represent reliably the extralinguistic world. His physical descriptions of character demonstrate most
convincingly the inverse relation between the amount of representation and the degree of confidence in the efficacy of representation: the
longest descriptions are generally the least exact, the most difficult
to visualize. Details challenge, contradict, and blur one another, so
that the longer the act of describing continues, the more uncertain it
appears. Ironically, given the illustrations that typically accompany
his texts and the frequency with which his novels have been adapted
into cinematic and theatrical forms, and contrary to popular wisdom,
Dickens's is among the most unvisualizable of novelistic worlds. Ren-
dering Dickens's descriptive language in visual terms necessarily means
making the possible definite, the contradictory compatible; it preserves
at least some of the particulars but alters the relationship among them
and erases Dickens's most characteristic signatures.

Thus the process of characterization in Dickens is one in which
the novelist attempts to understand an unstable internal life through
unreliable external signs and to convey his understanding through an
imperfect medium. This is not a bad way of describing the process
of characterization in general, and most of Dickens's important contemporaries would probably acknowledge, at least to some extent,
the relatively fragile foundation upon which that process rests. To
adapt Jaffe's argument, the elaborate attempts at characterization
in the nineteenth-century novel may be seen to reflect an increasing
uncertainty about the nature of character. Dickens differs from the
others not in kind but in degree, and especially in the anxious self-
referentiality of his depiction of character: even as he is engaged in
the process of characterization, he is scrutinizing and problematizing
that process. "Dickens does not want to make us see," writes Thomas
Docherty, "but to make us learn how to see" (and to recognize the
limitations of seeing); his gaze does not replace the reader's but in-
structs and sometimes clouds it.[6] As my consideration of *Little Dorrit*
has attempted to demonstrate, his novels are filled with reflections
on and parodies of their own descriptive language, with passages
in which covert concerns about characterization become overt, and
with images that encapsulate the elusiveness of personality. Regardless
of the positions taken by Dickens the man, who was not given to

6. Docherty, *(Absent) Character*, 19.

public shows of hesitation, Dickens the novelist was clearly alert to at least some of the contradictions and evasions embedded in his work. I would endorse Kate Flint's admonition "that in pointing to the contradictions in Dickens' writings we must not fall into the trap of thinking that their presence is always unconscious."[7] To do so is to overlook what those writings say about themselves.

Few words are more scrupulously avoided in contemporary criticism than the highly suspect "lifelike": from some theoretical perspectives literature is understood as wholly disconnected from "life," while from others it is understood as connected in ways too complicated to be represented by a term that begs so many questions. Nevertheless, it seems important to emphasize again the sense in which Dickens's characters seem to me most lifelike and convincing, in which, that is, they provoke in the reader a response most congruent with a response provoked by life outside the text. To a greater extent than most fictional characters, they seem to invite yet resist understanding. So much information seems available for apprehension—so many physical particulars, gestures, habits, words—yet, as with people in the world, so little proves to be definitive and unambiguous. What Baruch Hochman calls the "teleology" and "purposiveness" that distinguish fictional characters from "the personalities that we deal with in life" are in Dickens qualified by doubt and contradiction, so that reactions to the two come more closely to resemble one another.[8] Characters that seem initially to be thoroughly knowable prove in the end to be as present and absent, definite and indefinite, as shadows.

---

7. Flint, *Dickens*, 46. James A. Davies makes a similar point in discussing Dickens's "highly semiotic, textually-conscious, writerly art." See *Textual Life*, 4.
8. Hochman, *Character*, 69.

Bibliography

Ackroyd, Peter. *Dickens*. New York: HarperCollins, 1990.

Alexander, Doris. *Creating Characters with Charles Dickens*. University Park: Pennsylvania State University Press, 1991.

Altick, Richard D. *Presence of the Present: Topics of the Day in the Victorian Novel*. Columbus: Ohio State University Press, 1991.

Arac, Jonathan. "*Hamlet, Little Dorrit*, and the History of Character." *South Atlantic Quarterly* 87 (1988): 311–28.

Bagehot, Walter. "Charles Dickens." In *Charles Dickens: A Critical Anthology*. Edited by Stephen Wall. Baltimore: Penguin, 1970, 123–43.

Barthes, Roland. *Image, Music, Text*. Translated by Stephen Heath. New York: Hill and Wang, 1977.

———. *S/Z: An Essay*. Translated by Richard Miller. New York: Hill and Wang, 1974.

Bayley, John. *The Characters of Love: A Study in the Literature of Personality*. New York: Basic Books, 1960.

Belsey, Catherine. *Critical Practice*. New York: Methuen, 1980.

Berthoff, Warner. " 'Our Means Will Make Us Means': Character as Virtue in *Hamlet* and *All's Well*." *New Literary History* 5 (1974): 319–51.

Brontë, Charlotte. *Jane Eyre*. 1847. Reprint, New York: Penguin, 1966.

———. *Shirley*. 1849. Reprint, New York: Dutton, 1908.

Brook, G. L. *The Language of Dickens*. London: Andre Deutsch, 1970.

Brown, Marshall. "The Logic of Realism: A Hegelian Approach." *PMLA* 96 (1981): 224–41.

Browne, Edgar. *Phiz and Dickens*. London: James Nisbet and Co., 1913.

Bruner, Jerome. "The Narrative Construction of Reality." *Critical Inquiry* 18 (1991): 1–21.

Carey, John. *Here Comes Dickens: The Imagination of a Novelist*. New York: Schocken Books, 1973.

Carlisle, Janice M. "*Little Dorrit*: Necessary Fictions." *Studies in the Novel* 7 (1975): 195–214.

Carlyle, Thomas. *Selected Essays*. New York: Dutton, 1972.

Cecil, David. *Early Victorian Novelists*. London: Constable and Co., 1934.

Chase, Karen. *Eros and Psyche: The Representation of Personality in Charlotte Brontë, Charles Dickens, George Eliot*. New York: Methuen, 1984.

Chatman, Seymour. *Story and Discourse: Narrative Structure in Fiction and Film*. Ithaca: Cornell University Press, 1978.

Chesterton, G. K. *Charles Dickens*. 1906. Reprint, New York: Schocken Books, 1965.

———. "*The Pickwick Papers*." In *The Dickens Critics*. Edited by George H. Ford and Lauriat Lane Jr. Ithaca: Cornell University Press, 1961, 109–21.

Childers, Joseph W. "History, Totality, Opposition: The New Historicism and *Little Dorrit*." *Dickens Quarterly* 6 (1989): 150–57.

Cixous, Hélène. "The Character of 'Character.' " *New Literary History* 5 (1974): 383–402.

Clayton, Jay. "Dickens and the Genealogy of Postmodernism." *Nineteenth-Century Literature* 46 (1991): 181–95.

Cohen, Jane R. *Charles Dickens and His Original Illustrators*. Columbus: Ohio State University Press, 1980.

Colley, Ann C. *Tennyson and Madness*. Athens: University of Georgia Press, 1983.

Collins, Philip, ed. *Dickens: The Critical Heritage*. New York: Barnes and Noble, 1971.

Collins, Wilkie. Preface to *The Woman in White*. 2d ed. 1862. Reprint, New York: Penguin, 1974, 31–32.

Connor, Steven. *Charles Dickens*. New York: Basil Blackwell, 1985.

Culler, Jonathan. "Issues in Contemporary American Critical Debate." In *American Criticism in the Poststructuralist Age*. Edited by Ira Koningsberg. Ann Arbor: University of Michigan Press, 1981, 1–18.

———. *On Deconstruction: Theory and Criticism after Structuralism*. Ithaca: Cornell University Press, 1982.

———. *Structuralist Poetics: Structuralism, Linguistics, and the Study of Literature*. Ithaca: Cornell University Press, 1975.

Davies, James A. *The Textual Life of Dickens's Characters*. Savage, Md.: Barnes and Noble, 1990.

Davies, John D. *Phrenology Fad and Science: A 19th-Century American Crusade.* New Haven: Yale University Press, 1955.

Davis, Lennard J. *Factual Fictions: The Origins of the English Novel.* New York: Columbia University Press, 1983.

de Giustino, David. *Conquest of the Mind: Phrenology and Victorian Social Thought.* Totowa, N.J.: Rowman and Littlefield, 1975.

Dickens, Charles. *The Letters of Charles Dickens.* Vol. 6. Edited by Madeline House, Graham Storey, and Kathleen Tillotson. Oxford: Clarendon Press, 1988.

Docherty, Thomas. *Reading (Absent) Character: Towards a Theory of Characterization in Fiction.* Oxford: Clarendon Press, 1983.

Eagleton, Terry. *Literary Theory: An Introduction.* Minneapolis: University of Minnesota Press, 1983.

Eliot, George. *Daniel Deronda.* 1876. Reprint, Oxford: Clarendon Press, 1984.

———. *The George Eliot Letters.* Vol. 2. Edited by Gordon S. Haight. New Haven: Yale University Press, 1954.

———. *Middlemarch.* 1872. Reprint, Boston: Houghton Mifflin, 1956.

Eliot, T. S. "Wilkie Collins and Dickens." In *The Dickens Critics.* Edited by George H. Ford and Lauriat Lane Jr. Ithaca: Cornell University Press, 1961, 151–52.

Faas, Ekbert. *Retreat into the Mind: Victorian Poetry and the Rise of Psychiatry.* Princeton: Princeton University Press, 1988.

Fenstermaker, John J. *Charles Dickens, 1940–1975: An Analytical Subject Index to Periodical Criticism of the Novels and Christmas Books.* Boston: G. K. Hall, 1979.

Ferrara, Fernando. "Theory and Model for the Structural Analysis of Fiction." *New Literary History* 5 (1974): 245–68.

Flaxman, Rhonda L. *Victorian Word-Painting and Narrative: Toward the Blending of Genres.* Ann Arbor: U. M. I. Research Press, 1987.

Flint, Kate. *Dickens.* Atlantic Highlands, N.J.: Humanities Press International, 1988.

Foley, Barbara. *Telling the Truth: The Theory and Practice of Documentary Fiction.* Ithaca: Cornell University Press, 1986.

Ford, George H. *Dickens and His Readers: Aspects of Novel-Criticism since 1836.* Princeton: Princeton University Press, 1955.

Ford, George H., and Lauriat Lane Jr., eds. *The Dickens Critics.* Ithaca: Cornell University Press, 1961.

Forster, E. M. *Aspects of the Novel.* New York: Harcourt, Brace, 1927.

Forster, John. *The Life of Charles Dickens.* 3 vols. Philadelphia: J. B. Lippincott, 1872–1874.

Foucault, Michel. *The Order of Things: An Archeology of the Human Sciences.* New York: Random House, 1970.

Fulweiler, Howard W. " 'A Dismal Swamp': Darwin, Design, and Evolution in *Our Mutual Friend.*" *Nineteenth-Century Literature* 49 (1994): 50–74.

Garis, Robert. *The Dickens Theatre: A Reassessment of the Novels.* Oxford: Clarendon Press, 1965.

Gass, William. *Fiction and the Figures of Life.* New York: Alfred A. Knopf, 1970.

Gillman, Susan K., and Robert L. Patten. "Dickens: Doubles:: Twain: Twins." *Nineteenth-Century Fiction* 39 (1985): 441–58.

Gissing, George. *Charles Dickens.* 1898. Reprint, Port Washington, N.Y.: Kennikat Press, 1966.

Glancy, Ruth. "Dickens at Work on *The Haunted Man.*" *Dickens Studies Annual* 15 (1986): 65–86.

Gold, Joseph. *The Stature of Dickens: A Centenary Bibliography.* Toronto: University of Toronto Press, 1971.

Gombrich, E. H. *Meditations on a Hobby Horse and Other Essays on the Theory of Art.* London: Phaidon Press, 1963.

Gross, John, and Gabriel Pearson, eds. *Dickens and the Twentieth Century.* Toronto: University of Toronto Press, 1962.

Guerard, Albert. "The Illuminating Distortion." *Novel* 5 (1972): 101–21.

Harvey, John R. *Victorian Novelists and Their Illustrators.* New York: New York University Press, 1971.

Harvey, W. J. *Character and the Novel.* Ithaca: Cornell University Press, 1965.

Herst, Beth F. *The Dickens Hero: Selfhood and Alienation in the Dickens World.* New York: St. Martin's Press, 1990.

Higbie, Robert. *Character and Structure in the English Novel.* Gainesville: University of Florida Press, 1984.

Hochman, Baruch. *Character in Literature.* Ithaca: Cornell University Press, 1985.

Hollington, Michael. "The Live Hieroglyphic: Physiologie and Physiognomy in *Martin Chuzzlewit.*" *Dickens Quarterly* 10 (1993): 57–68.

Holoch, George. "Consciousness and Society in *Little Dorrit*." *Victorian Studies* 21 (1978): 335–51.

Horne, R. H. *A New Spirit of the Age*. New York, 1844.

Horton, Susan R. *Interpreting Interpreting: Interpreting Dickens's Dombey*. Baltimore: Johns Hopkins University Press, 1979.

———. *The Reader in the Dickens World: Style and Response*. Pittsburgh: University of Pittsburgh Press, 1981.

Houghton, Walter. *The Victorian Frame-of-Mind 1830–1870*. New Haven: Yale University Press, 1957.

Howells, William Dean. *Criticism and Fiction and Other Essays*. New York: New York University Press, 1959.

Hutton, Richard Holt. *Criticisms on Contemporary Thought and Thinkers: Selections from* The Spectator. London, 1894.

Huxley, Aldous. "The Vulgarity of Little Nell." In *The Dickens Critics*. Edited by George H. Ford and Lauriat Lane Jr. Ithaca: Cornell University Press, 1961, 153–56.

Jaffe, Audrey. *Vanishing Points: Dickens, Narrative, and the Subject of Omniscience*. Berkeley: University of California Press, 1991.

Jakobson, Roman, and Morris Halle. *Fundamentals of Language*. The Hague: Mouton and Co., 1956.

James, Henry. *Theory of Fiction*. Edited by James E. Miller Jr. Lincoln: University of Nebraska Press, 1982.

Johnson, E. D. H. *Charles Dickens: An Introduction to His Novels*. New York: Random House, 1969.

Kaplan, Fred. "The Development of Dickens' Style." Ph.D. diss., Columbia University, 1966.

———. *Dickens: A Biography*. New York: William Morrow, 1988.

———. *Dickens and Mesmerism: The Hidden Springs of Fiction*. Princeton: Princeton University Press, 1975.

Kernan, Alvin. *The Death of Literature*. New Haven: Yale University Press, 1990.

Kincaid, James R. *Dickens and the Rhetoric of Laughter*. Oxford: Clarendon Press, 1971.

———. "Performance, Roles, and the Nature of the Self." In *Dramatic Dickens*. Edited by Carol Hanbury Mackay. New York: St. Martin's Press, 1989, 11–26.

———. "Viewing and Blurring in Dickens: The Misrepresentation of Representation." *Dickens Studies Annual* 16 (1987): 95–111.

Knights, L. C. "How Many Children Had Lady Macbeth?" Cambridge: G. Fraser, 1933.

Kucich, John. "Recent Dickens Studies: 1989." *Dickens Studies Annual* 20 (1991): 313–60.

——. *Repression in Victorian Fiction: Charlotte Brontë, George Eliot, and Charles Dickens*. Berkeley: University of California Press, 1987.

Lankford, William T. " 'The Parish Boy's Progress': The Evolving Form of *Oliver Twist*." *PMLA* 93 (1978): 20–32.

Larson, Janet L. *Dickens and the Broken Scripture*. Athens: University of Georgia Press, 1985.

Leavis, F. R., and Q. D. Leavis. *Dickens the Novelist*. London: Chatto and Windus, 1970.

Leavis, Q. D. *Fiction and the Reading Public*. London: Chatto and Windus, 1932.

Lecker, Barbara. "The Split Characters of Charles Dickens." *Studies in English Literature* 19 (1979): 689–704.

Lettis, Richard. *Dickens on Literature: A Continuing Study of His Aesthetic*. New York: AMS Press, 1990.

Levine, George. "By Knowledge Possessed: Darwin, Nature, and Victorian Narrative." *New Literary History* 24 (1993): 363–91.

——. *Darwin and the Novelists: Patterns of Science in Victorian Fiction*. Cambridge: Harvard University Press, 1988.

——. "Realism Reconsidered." In *The Theory of the Novel: New Essays*. Edited by John Halperin. New York: Oxford University Press, 1974, 233–56.

——. *The Realistic Imagination: English Fiction from Frankenstein to Lady Chatterley*. Chicago: University of Chicago Press, 1981.

Lewes, George Henry. "Dickens in Relation to Criticism." In *The Dickens Critics*. Edited by George H. Ford and Lauriat Lane Jr. Ithaca: Cornell University Press, 1961, 54–73.

Lucas, John. *The Melancholy Man: A Study of Dickens's Novels*. 2d ed. New Jersey: Barnes and Noble, 1980.

Machen, Arthur. "The Art of Dickens." *The Academy*, April 11, 1908, 666.

Manning, Sylvia. "Social Criticism and Textual Subversion in *Little Dorrit*." *Dickens Studies Annual* 20 (1991): 127–46.

Marcus, Steven. *Dickens: From Pickwick to Dombey*. New York: Simon and Schuster, 1965.

McGann, Jerome J. *The Beauty of Inflections: Literary Investigations in Historical Method and Theory*. Oxford: Clarendon Press, 1988.

McKeon, Michael. *The Origins of the English Novel 1600–1740*. Baltimore: Johns Hopkins University Press, 1987.

McKnight, Natalie. *Idiots, Madmen, and Other Prisoners in Dickens.* New York: St. Martin's Press, 1993.

McMaster, Juliet. "Diabolic Trinity in *Oliver Twist.*" *Dalhousie Review* 61 (1981): 263–77.

———. *Dickens the Designer.* Totowa, N.J.: Barnes and Noble, 1987.

Meisel, Martin. *Realizations: Narrative, Pictorial, and Theatrical Arts in Nineteenth-Century England.* Princeton: Princeton University Press, 1983.

Melville, Herman. *The Piazza Tales and Other Prose Pieces.* Edited by Harrison Hayford, Alma A. MacDougall, and G. Thomas Tanselle. Evanston and Chicago: Northwestern University Press and The Newberry Library, 1987.

Menand, Louis. "What Are Universities For?" In *Falling into Theory: Conflicting Views on Reading Literature.* Edited by David H. Richter. Boston: St. Martin's Press, 1994, 88–99.

Metz, Nancy Aycock. "The Blighted Tree and the Book of Fate: Female Models of Storytelling in *Little Dorrit.*" *Dickens Studies Annual* 18 (1989): 221–41.

Miller, D. A. *The Novel and the Police.* Berkeley: University of California Press, 1988.

Miller, J. Hillis. *Charles Dickens: The World of His Novels.* Cambridge: Harvard University Press, 1958.

Monod, Sylvère. "Some Stylistic Devices in *A Tale of Two Cities.*" In *Dickens the Craftsman: Strategies of Presentation.* Edited by Robert B. Partlow Jr. Carbondale: Southern Illinois University Press, 1970, 165–86.

Moynahan, Julian. "The Hero's Guilt: The Case of *Great Expectations.*" *Essays in Criticism* 10 (1960): 60–79.

Myers, Walter L. *The Later Realism: A Study of Characterization in the British Novel.* Chicago: University of Chicago Press, 1927.

Newcomb, Mildred. *The Imagined World of Charles Dickens.* Columbus: Ohio State University Press, 1989.

Newsome, Robert. *Dickens on the Romantic Side of Familiar Things: Bleak House and the Novel Tradition.* New York: Columbia University Press, 1977.

O'Faolain, Sean. *The English Novel.* Edited by Derek Verschoyle. New York: Harcourt, Brace, 1936.

Ortega y Gasset, José. *The Dehumanization of Art and Other Essays on Art, Culture, and Literature.* Translated by Helene Weyl. Princeton: Princeton University Press, 1948.

Orwell, George. *A Collection of Essays*. New York: Harcourt, Brace, 1946.

Paroissien, David. "Recent Dickens Studies: 1986." *Dickens Studies Annual* 17 (1988): 317–71.

Pater, Walter. *The Renaissance*. 1873. Reprint, Chicago: Academy Press, 1977.

Phelan, James. *Reading People, Reading Plots: Character, Progression, and the Interpretation of Narrative*. Chicago: University of Chicago Press, 1989.

Poe, Edgar Allan. *"The Old Curiosity Shop."* In *The Dickens Critics*. Edited by George H. Ford and Lauriat Lane Jr. Ithaca: Cornell University Press, 1961, 19–24.

Price, Martin. *Forms of Life: Character and Moral Imagination in the Novel*. New Haven: Yale University Press, 1983.

———. "The Logic of Intensity: More on Character." *Critical Inquiry* 2 (1975): 369–79.

Raina, Badri. *Dickens and the Dialectic of Growth*. Madison: University of Wisconsin Press, 1986.

Reid, J. C. *Charles Dickens: Little Dorrit*. London: Edward Arnold, 1967.

Richards, I. A. *Principles of Literary Criticism*. New York: Harcourt, Brace, 1925.

Roberts, Paul. *Understanding Grammar*. New York: Harper and Row, 1954.

Romano, John. *Dickens and Reality*. New York: Columbia University Press, 1978.

Rosenberg, Brian. "The Language of Doubt in *Oliver Twist*." *Dickens Quarterly* 4 (1987): 91–99.

———. "Physical Opposition in *Barnaby Rudge*." *Victorian Newsletter* 67 (1985): 21–22.

Saintsbury, George. *Corrected Impressions: Essays on Victorian Writers*. London: Heinemann, 1895.

Santayana, George. "Dickens." In *The Dickens Critics*. Edited by George H. Ford and Lauriat Lane Jr. Ithaca: Cornell University Press, 1961, 135–50.

Shaw, George Bernard. *"Hard Times."* In *The Dickens Critics*. Edited by George H. Ford and Lauriat Lane Jr. Ithaca: Cornell University Press, 1961, 125–34.

Sheridan, Daniel. "The Unreadable *Dombey*." *Dickens Quarterly* 6 (1989): 142–49.

Showalter, Elaine. "Guilt, Authority, and the Shadows of *Little Dorrit*." *Nineteenth-Century Fiction* 34 (1979): 20–40.

Simpson, David. *Fetishism and Imagination: Dickens, Melville, Conrad*. Baltimore: Johns Hopkins University Press, 1982.

Smith, Grahame. *Dickens, Money, and Society*. Berkeley: University of California Press, 1968.

Squires, Michael. "The Structure of Dickens's Imagination in *Little Dorrit*." *Texas Studies in Literature and Language* 30 (1988): 49–64.

Steig, Michael. *Dickens and Phiz*. Bloomington: Indiana University Press, 1978.

Stoehr, Taylor. *Dickens: The Dreamer's Stance*. Ithaca: Cornell University Press, 1965.

Stone, Harry. *Dickens and the Invisible World: Fairy Tale, Fantasy, and Novel-Making*. Bloomington: Indiana University Press, 1979.

Thomas, Deborah A. *Dickens and the Short Story*. Philadelphia: University of Pennsylvania Press, 1982.

Tillotson, Geoffrey. Introduction to *Villette*. By Charlotte Brontë. Boston: Houghton, Mifflin, 1971, v–xviii.

Tompkins, Jane P., ed. *Reader-Response Criticism: From Formalism to Post-Structuralism*. Baltimore: Johns Hopkins University Press, 1980.

Trilling, Lionel. Introduction to *Little Dorrit*. By Charles Dickens. New York: Oxford University Press, 1953, v–xvi.

Trollope, Anthony. *Autobiography*. 1883. Reprint, New York: Dodd, Mead, 1927.

Vogel, Jane. *Allegory in Dickens*. University: University of Alabama Press, 1977.

Wain, John. *"Little Dorrit."* In *Dickens and the Twentieth Century*. Edited by John Gross and Gabriel Pearson. Toronto: University of Toronto Press, 1962, 175–86.

Wall, Stephen, ed. *Charles Dickens: A Critical Anthology*. Baltimore: Penguin, 1970.

Ward, A. W. *Dickens*. London, 1882.

Watkins, Gwen. *Dickens in Search of Himself: Recurrent Themes and Characters in the Works of Charles Dickens*. Totowa, N.J.: Barnes and Noble, 1987.

Weinsheimer, Joel. "Theory of Character: *Emma*." *Poetics Today* 1 (1979): 185–211.

Weinstein, Philip M. *The Semantics of Desire: Changing Models of*

Identity from Dickens to Joyce. Princeton: Princeton University Press, 1984.

Welsh, Alexander. *The City of Dickens*. Oxford: Clarendon Press, 1971.

———. *From Copyright to Copperfield: The Identity of Dickens*. Cambridge: Harvard University Press, 1987.

Wilde, Alan. "Mr. F's Aunt and the Analogical Structure of *Little Dorrit*." *Nineteenth-Century Fiction* 19 (1964): 33–44.

Wills, Gary. "Dorrit without Politics." *New York Review of Books*, February 2, 1989: 16–18.

Wilson, Edmund. *The Wound and the Bow: Seven Studies in Literature*. Cambridge, Mass.: Houghton, Mifflin, 1941.

Winters, Warrington. "Dickens and the Psychology of Dreams." *PMLA* 63 (1948): 984–1006.

Yeazell, Ruth Bernard. "Do It or Dorrit." *Novel* 25 (1991): 33–49.

INDEX

Allegory, 38, 113, 123
Altick, Richard, 99
Analogy, in Dickens, 60
Arac, Jonathan, 4, 47
Arnold, Matthew: "Dover Beach,"
28; "Empedocles on Etna," 94;
mentioned, 28, 94, 97, 101

Bagehot, Walter, 54, 67
Balzac, Honoré de, 18
Barnaby Rudge (Dickens): imagery in,
120–21; mentioned, 47, 71, 107
—characters: Chester, Edward, 71,
105, 107; Chester, John, 120–21;
Daisy, Solomon, 142; Gashford,
71; Haredale, Emma, 120–21;
Haredale, Geoffrey, 120; Hugh,
107, 121; Rudge, Barnaby, 104,
107, 121, 140; Tappertit, Sim, 107,
121; Varden, Dolly, 120–21; Varden,
Gabriel, 120; Willet, Joe, 107
Barrett, Elizabeth, 97
Barth, John, 85
Barthes, Roland, 2, 3, 131
Bayley, John, 17, 77, 79
Beadnell, Maria, 39
Belsey, Catherine, 2–3, 140, 145–46
Berthoff, Warner, 9–10
Blake, William, 94
Bleak House (Dickens): critical
reception of, 33; narrators of,
74–75; mentioned, 32, 34, 43, 47,
49, 113
—characters: Bucket, Inspector, 142,
143; Dedlock, Lady, 75; Flite, Miss,
140; Guster, 140; Jellyby, Mrs., 78;
Krook, Mr., 75; Smallweed, Mrs.,
140; Summerson, Esther, 43, 74–75,
104, 123; Tulkinghorn, Mr., 142;
Turveydrop, Mr., 75
Brontë, Charlotte: and phrenology,
98–99; *Jane Eyre*, 94–95; *Shirley*,
99; mentioned, 111

Brook, G. L., 56
Brown, Marshall, 146
Browne, Hablot K. (Phiz), 49–53
Browning, Robert: "Mesmerism," 97;
mentioned, 94, 97
Bruner, Jerome, 12
Bulwer-Lytton, Edward, 98
Byron, George Gordon, Lord, 94

Carey, John, 113
Carlisle, Janice, 89
Carlyle, Thomas, 17, 32, 100
Cecil, David, 15, 20, 27, 78
Chase, Karen, 26, 67, 85, 86, 101, 147
Chatman, Seymour, 111, 133, 138
Chekhov, Anton, 119
Chesterton, G. K., 18
Chimes, The (Dickens), 74
Christmas Carol, A (Dickens): Scrooge,
Ebenezer, 123, 134; mentioned, 74,
134
Cixous, Hélène, 1, 2, 9–10, 11
Clayton, Jay, 85
Clough, Arthur Hugh, 97
Cohen, Jane R., 49–50
Colley, Ann, 95–96, 100
Collins, Philip, 32, 33
Collins, Wilkie, 20
Combe, George, 98
Connor, Steven, 21, 131, 132
Culler, Jonathan, 29, 131–32, 137

Dante, 18
Darwin, Charles, 40, 100
David Copperfield (Dickens), 32, 34,
48, 58, 105, 107–8, 122
—characters: Copperfield, David,
58, 74, 107, 108, 110; Dick,
Mr., 140; Heep, Uriah, 107, 108,
109; Micawber, Wilkins, 19, 78;
Steerforth, James, 107; Trotwood,
Betsey, 140; Wickfield, Agnes, 107
Davies, James, 47, 67

161